1970

This book may be kept

FOURTEEN DAYS

BEYOND INDIVIDUALITY

BEYOND
INDIVIDUALITY

by CLINTON R. MEEK

PHILOSOPHICAL LIBRARY
New York

Library of Congress Catalog Card No. 78-103282

SBN 8022-2320-6

PRINTED IN THE UNITED STATES OF AMERICA

Contents

Chapter

/ I. VIEW OF INDIVIDUALITY 1

II. EXISTENTIALISM AND ZEN 10

/ III. IDENTITY 20

/ IV. SELF-VALIDATION 29

/ V. SELF-REALIZATION AND SELF-ACTUALIZATION 39

/ VI. RESPONSIVENESS AND RESPONSIBILITY 47

VII. CONFORMITY AND CREATIVITY 56

VIII. LEISURE AND WORK 66

IX. MEANING AND VALUE 75

X. PSYCHOTHERAPY 85

Bibliography 96

Preface

In discussing individuality, I feel as though I were standing before a Zen master who demands that I speak up to reveal reality, but I know before I start that I shall receive thirty blows whether or not I speak. I cannot hope to be very articulate in face of the demand. However, the urgency of the demand will not let me remain silent.

This is a book to encourage the individual to develop himself beyond the conventional level of existence. The open side of individuality with its possibilities is stressed. The individual is encouraged to be flexible in his point of view so as to include as much of his reality as possible; consciousness can be progressively open to include more and more of reality. I am in full agreement with many of the writers who are striving to integrate Eastern and Western thought for a better balanced view of the whole man. I have used Existentialism as the most comprehensive view of man in the Western tradition in which the primary emphasis has been on actualizing oneself through the development of one's potentials. I have used Zen as representative of the Eastern approach where realization of one's ground of being is emphasized.

CHAPTER I

View of Individuality

Almost any view of man is possible. He is first of all potential in a world of opportunity. The greatest of his potentials is mind, which lights the way as he enters the world using his other potentials. Each particular mind sees the potentials of one's being and of the world that it finds itself in, in the way in which it projects itself. Each projects himself and constitutes himself according to his purpose. The mind is intentional.

It has been demonstrated in history that man can see himself and other men in an indeterminable number of ways. It would be difficult, if not impossible, to determine how many philosophical and religious systems there have been to view the nonsubstantial side of existence, explaining, at the same time, the empirical side of existence, usually as a temporary passing phenomenon.

There have been numerous psychologies to explain the more substantial side of man, generally explaining the nonsubstantial side of man as essentially unreal. Many theories have centered on the interaction of these two aspects of existence. Each man, through history, has had his own view, always a complete view, but not orderly enough to be called a system. It is safe to say that even each person that closely followed a system had his own personal interpretation, even if he used the same words to conceptualize it.

All of these explanations of man have some truth in them, in that they point to some aspect of reality, no matter how distorted their abstractions from reality may have been. The complexities

1

of appearance of reality are illustrated by the analogy of Indra's Net: An endless net of threads filling the universe is visualized. The horizontal threads extend in space, the vertical threads extend in time. At every crossing of threads is an individual, represented by a crystal bead. The bright light of Being illuminates and penetrates every crystal bead; but also every bead reflects the light from every other crystal in the net, as well as every reflection of every reflection throughout the universe.

It is reasonable to conclude that any theory is not inclusive enough to cover the complexity of existence. The mind of the individual transcends these systems and whatever reality they point to; the mind can take any point of view and, thus, see the truth in different reflections. The usual approach has been to adopt one view and nihilate all the rest of reality, for the sake of security. However, there is a possibility that even greater security is provided if man freely uses all views open to him. There is more security to be found in freedom than there is to be found in a bound unit which constantly struggles to maintain its artificial boundary. At first it might appear that to recognize the limitation of a point of view of oneself as being only partial might undermine confidence in having an adequate identity of oneself. But the reverse is true. In utilizing all his different views one comes to know himself in much the same way as he comes to know his friends, his car, or his house. If he does not see that he is many different things, and that many of them can possibly be conflicting, he must limit himself to what is always true. In this case, all impermanent phenomena lose their reality.

In considering the reality of the individual (or the individual's reality), the point of view of the viewer is the starting point. One, as the viewer, is always in a particular place and in a particular psychological state of the moment; both of these are unique at the time of any observation. The viewer is common to all points of view, and he has the capacity to unify different views. Each view, if clearly seen is always true, but only from that point of view. The whole truth would depend on all possible views. The person as the viewer does not change with each view, but the response he makes is according to what is viewed.

One can view himself according to the guidance of a theoretical view of man. And whatever view one takes will be a guide to how he sees himself in the world and the action he will take; hence, how he actualizes himself. For example, he can take a poetic, psychological, religious, or functional view of himself.

The shifting of the point of view is a free process. The individual has freedom to transcend in many ways any actuality which he encounters. There is something substantial about him as long as he lives, having a body and observable functions. There is just as definitely his nonsubstantial consciousness which deals with all that comes before it, but it cannot deal with itself in the same way. There are many subsystems or subpatterns from which he judges. And, of course, there is the reality of interactions and mobility in his field. All of life, therefore, cannot be placed in any conceptual order. The proper way to understand life is in no stopping of this mobile viewpoint, and there is no systematic pattern that this shifting point of view must follow, nor can conceptualization keep pace with it.

The individual is the source of all significance, all meaning and value, and all that is known and constructed by man. Man's outstanding characteristic is his ability to understand, to come to know, to set forces in action in the light of his mind which is formed by this process. The individual lives his life through this process of arising in understanding, differentiating in light of understanding to obtain knowledge of how things can be controlled, and then acting and setting other forces into action to achieve his end. Conventional reality is the product of this life-process.

One lives by encounter in experience, and this is the basis of his reality. All meanings and values are inherent in concrete experience according to differentiations made. One develops himself within the conventions of his society, but adequate individualization will depend on his own initiative. Orientation for identity must be shifted from conventional reality to individual reality. After gaining independence from the conventions and realizing his interdependence in reality, the individual must still live in the conventions much as he did while he was dominated by the conventions. However, his personal life and his creative projection into the conventional forms will differ greatly in the quality of his experience. He may fit himself into a system, or he may have an

3

open approach in developing understanding of reality. Consistency is not required because the individual does not have a fixed nature; he is a life-process, but bound to a life-process pattern only biologically. As psychological process he is free and open. He must accept freedom and responsibility if he is to develop his individuality beyond the conventional level of the masses. There may be a movement from the conventions of society to the reality of the culture. And from the reality of the culture he may move to direct connections with cosmic reality.

Human individuality is the source of all human reality. By human reality is meant all that man has accomplished, all that he has added to the world and the understanding and knowledge that he has developed. It consists of the conventional reality and the human quality within man. The Self or Mind is cosmic reality. Self is the light in which the human mind (as a particular mind in each) is developed. The progress that has been made depended on man binding together to give the cumulative efforts of all individuals who have contributed or who have acted to confirm human reality.

The basis of humanity depends upon the binding of humanity into an interdependent body. The absolute dependency of the infant is the source of the mature adult becoming interdependent. It is a mistake to say that he becomes independent. This dependency in infancy brings intensification of care to the point of differentiation into love and, of course, hate. Love and hate are the bases of the vigor which enabled man to establish his human reality. Love is basic to his getting and having, and hate is basic to his destroying and removing whatever interferes with his project (of establishing his own reality).

In the socialization process the individual begins life as a helpless infant. His life depends on the significant persons around him. His helplessness inspires love and his gratitude and absolute need for others inspires love for him. This love is the basis of the individual's humanity, his ability to care for others in a positive way and to accept their reality. The dependency upon others, and the love that develops along with it, provide the strong motivation needed to imitate others and to learn rapidly through consensual validation. The person, thus, acquires the conventional conscious

4

structure of his society, learning to use the language and to conceptualize reality the way the society does, and acquiring the conventional meaning and values.

The socialization process is vital; it is the process through which the individual is created as a human, but there is grave danger in his coming to conform. To escape conformity, the rediscovery of individuality for its sharper interaction with humanity is necessary. If the individual remains one of the masses, he contributes to the stability of humanity, but he does not contribute to its progress in furthering interaction with the cosmos. Revolutionaries may bring change instead of progress; such change frequently delays and disrupts true progress. True progress concerns the quality of humanness and not the organization of society, or its industrialization. It is in direct authentic interaction and through authentic communication that human progress is made.

The individualized person behaves conventionally, when it does not interfere with his authentic expression. When there is conflict with conventions, the creative person should have more ingenuity in using the conventional form than the masses do when they are in conflict. The authentic person takes responsibility for helping to stabilize society. A society that changes too rapidly may create difficulties for the creative person; he needs the convention to be stable and dependable, to allow for personal freedom and flexibility.

The origin and ultimate of man is openness in awareness, but man lives life on the relative level, with the actual beings and in the actual conditions of the world. Man had to develop his conscious contents and his ability to cope with living in the actual world. But just as the origin of man was in the openness in awareness, it is also the origin of the individual which is present in every moment of his waking life. Man was unconscious, he developed consciousness. In unconsciousness he is directly connected with reality; he came to know in consciousness by abstract representations of differentiations. After he has observed the conscious structure, he can see the unconscious as a background. We learn to know something before we can know of nothingness. We know we sleep by our being awake. After consciousness is created, we turn to the unconscious, out of which it came, to make it conscious.

But to make the unconscious conscious, consciousness must take the form of the unconscious; it makes itself flexible, soft, passive, responsive, and attains a state of leisure that it may know the unconscious. This is self-realization.

We are essentially sensitive openness which receives and responds. It is our sensitiveness which is activated. We have a minimum of power to act, but because of our sensitiveness for understanding and knowing, we are able to use our power in an enlightened way and to increase it through tools and instruments. We also set powerful forces we can control into action.

The sense of being a separate unit, the private person, has to be developed before it can be transcended. The separate self and the conscious mind are stepping stones. They are as tangible as it is possible to make them. It is after experiencing the limitations and the confines of this separate self that it becomes possible to experience the absolute freedom of transcending this separate unity. True freedom of reality is realized by leaving behind the limited self. Identity is shifted to reality itself; one comes to recognize that he is reality. It is the finite which makes the sense of the infinite possible, it gives an opposite for interaction. Beyond finite limitations (at the level of particular being) is the absolute identity of the opposites, Nishida has said.

The individual is a finite being who must live and interact on the actual level with particular things and forces. He has his basic needs on this level to take care of. Is not this enough to be concerned with? Why can man not let it go at this? This is an honest question and a wise one. But man transcends and is never entirely content with satisfying his basic needs. Give him everything he wants, and he continues to want. Sartre is right here, man is always lacking and continuing the search, wisely or unwisely. He usually works to satisfy his basic needs, but not always. Some individuals refuse to work, wanting something more, even from scratch. Most do work to satisfy basic needs, but even these are still not content with letting it go at that. They continue to struggle in destructive if not constructive directions. Man will not be satisfied or contained. He overflows all limits and all bounds, demanding his freedom, even if only to abuse or deny the very freedom he has demanded. Man always demands more than he is or has, even if he is unwilling to make the effort to get it. Perhaps the basis of his making demands that exceed his willingness to exert himself comes from his having been given, and always existing in the state of being given, the greatest prize of all from the mystery of Being. Man likes to take it easy and amuse himself the best and easiest way he can, but he always demands the best no matter how lax he has been. This does not deny that man also suffers anxiety, guilt, and despair because he does not put forth more effort.

The mind is reality. The organismic unit is reality. The mind is nothingness. It is nonsubstantial. The organismic unit belongs to the natural world and is the "somethingness" of reality. The organismic unit can use the mind to light itself and the world, and in this light, it can arrange things on its own. This is the source of cultures and civilizations, and it is the source of the individual.

Some say that the nothingness by which we are stopped at the mind is the ultimate reality. Most Eastern thought holds that all phenomena are only illusions. Others say that the "somethingness" is reality and there really is nothing else. They are realists or materialists. This seems to be the position of Western civilization. In the West, the nothingness was called soul and given a lot of attention for a while, but eventually it was forgotten by most. Attention was focused on "somethingness" until the aspect of the mind that deals with it was the only mind remembered. The original mind was forgotten. In the East, this original mind transcends all, and is said to activate all phenomena on the relative level.

Of mind nothing can be said except that it is open and within it differentiations are made and these differentiations can be related and organized. The mind is open to permit understanding, understanding encompasses differentiations. Mind has this power to transcend in understanding, and it has power to enter into concentrated attention to analyze, differentiate, and organize. This mind which enters into concentration of analyses to make differences and relates them is what we ordinarily call the conscious mind. It is connected with man who actualizes himself in whatever way he does. The transcending and understanding mind does not become this conscious mind; rather it is ground of this mind. It is called No-Mind in Zen. It is sensed in self-realization.

On the becoming or actualizing level, one is a knowing unit with energy and capacity to pursue whatever projects his capacity and the nature of his world permit. He unfolds through the interaction of knowledge and action; goals are selected and energy is channeled in his actions to become whatever he is to become.

Self-realization is of being, and self-actualization is becoming. When identified with being all that is needed is what is necessary for existence. One does only what he must, for anything else interferes with realization of being. Expressions beyond necessity are useless. Endless activity brings attention to activities which end in achievement, and then achievement and its results claim one's identity; thus, one becomes alienated from his true nature. In the East even the necessity has been neglected, to some extent. In the West the necessity has been exaggerated. The necessary action for the service of existence is enough—too much is dangerous. Man's whole project seems unnecessary, there is no place for it to lead, and it looks as if unconsciously realizing this, it is going to destroy itself.

Man has freedom to shape himself in whatever he actually makes of himself. He has freedom to create a mental representation of what he is. Of the complexities, of what may be differentiated within reality, there is no end. Of ways of actualizing and theories about it, there is no end, nor would there be any end as to what Being is if man could differentiate it, but it is too elusive, and, therefore, talking about it is only talk.

Man has being. He exists. In this existence he has freedom. As he actualizes himself he becomes an individual. Individuality has to do with this process of becoming an individual. Beyond individuality refers to the existence from which the individual makes himself stand out according to his projects. The beyond referred to here is in the totality of what one is as an essential part of the universe in which he is intrinsically embedded. The ground as Being encompasses the particular individual that one is becoming.

Individuality as seen on the conventional level is a stepping stone to the informal reality beyond the tangible. Free from the restrictions imposed on a substantial being, true identity is in the freedom beyond the substantial. Self transcends all particulars in

8

its openness as undifferentiated reality. Beyond the confines of the tangible world into the secret mysteries of Being, the nonsubstantial self is not only free but is the prime mover. The despair of the existentialists arises because the individual is not able to free himself from the limitations of the tangible side of existence. He is still too dependent upon the actual for satisfaction. Zen does somewhat better, but to get rid of the dominance of the substantial, all particulars are called impermanent illusions. With "things" and the reality of "things" put aside, the self that arises in self-realization is not subject to limitations and restrictions.

The realized self is beyond individuality. Before self-realization one thinks he will add measure to measure to fulfill his individuality. He expects to become more significant as an individual, but in the end, he finds this is not true. He comes to see beyond this individuality, comes to see its limitations, and he comes to see that it is by this individuality that all things are possible, if he can give it up, it opens up to Being and to the whole of reality. He comes to see that he belongs not simply within his individuality but to the totality of Being. At this point he is essentially beyond individuality. All things are possible, but not all things can be actualized. This is accepted. Only that which is readily actualized, without having to give up the basic sense of unformulated self, should be actualized. Just as one does not have to conceptualize the sunset to enjoy it, or the trees or the sky, one does not have to actualize reality to interact in it. To want to actualize all that one realizes is a form of greed. To actualize all is against the nature of things; it does not belong to the realm of the possible.

Individuality has established itself in history, in Western and Eastern fashion. Existentialism and Zen are two approaches to radical individualism. Existentialism has developed from Western thought to correct the bias of man getting shoved out of the picture which favors objective reality and forgets Being. Zen has developed from Eastern thought. In the West identity has been primarily with self-actualization; in the East identity has been primarily with the nonsubstantial realized self. It is the theme in this book that identity must be broad enough to include the whole man; both Western and Eastern views must be synthesized in the balance that best suits each individual. Self-realization and self-actualization are two major modes of our existence.

9

CHAPTER II

Existentialism and Zen

The East and the West have conceptualized individuality in drastically different ways. The West has come to visualize the individual as the separate ego who must somehow overcome his alienation to relate himself to reality for the satisfaction of his needs or the achievement of his goals. The East has visualized the individual as a manifestation of a Universal Self whose aim is to find his way back to identity with this Self.

Existentialism is one of the West's latest approaches to the problem of individuality. Its primary theme is that Western man has focused on objective reality and has neglected the problem of existence. Thus, the individual finds himself in his subjective existence to be greatly questioned in comparison with the tangible reality to which he has given his attention. Man has lost his place in nature and is surplus. There is no God to turn to for guidance. Man, thus, is a subjective creature with no true identity, as compared with the objective reality he has discovered by his scientific methods. Since he has no objective identity, it is up to him to make of himself whatever he is to be. The individual is to solve his problem of existence by finding his way back to the given phenomenon before the dualistic split which isolates the person from his world. He is to recognize his basic condition of being inseparably interwoven in the world and take responsibility as to how he actualizes himself and his world. He finds himself in the world according to the meaning and values he creates in his relationship with differentiated reality, as he conceptualizes and acts.

Heidegger emphasizes that man is primarily his possibilities, but Sartre insists that man is only what he determines himself to be in his actions. In either case, he is fully responsible and is condemned to freedom, with the necessity of choice and guilt to the extent that he does not fulfill his potential.

Zen is one of the East's latest approaches to the problem of individuality. It started in India with the teachings of Buddha, was taken to China where it became greatly modified by Taoism, and was later taken up by the Japanese. Recently it has received considerable attention in America. Zen demands that the individual realize his existence as his reality beyond the level of conceptual differentiations. For this reason Zen exists only in the living individual, before his experience is differentiated into dualistic thought; it cannot be adequately verbalized. The Zen approach grows out of the ancient conception of Universal Self postulated in the *Vedanta,* as interpreted by the Buddha. Brahma is the Universal Mind (ultimate reality); Atman which is the ultimate reality within the individual is a manifestation of Brahma, and the two are identical. Zen prefers the term "Universal Self," "Self," or "No-Mind." The aim of Zen is through practice to achieve enlightenment, which is called satori. Generally in English it is called self-realization. The ultimate in individuality is self-realization, which only incidentally requires actualization in expression. The emphasis is on realization and actualization is strictly secondary, although necessary as realization cannot exist without some form. The infinite can be expressed only in the finite, but no particular finite expression is necessarily preferable, as long as it genuinely expresses reality.

Existentialism emphasizes that the individual is open, free, and his actualization is up to him. The individual comes into this life with possibilities which enable him to create himself within the limits he finds in the nature of things. His own reality as a human is not incorporated in the scheme of the natural world. His having lived makes no difference except what little temporary difference it makes to the human world. Man's true significance is in his living his life according to his possibilities as he actualizes them. He finds himself existing in relation to things in the world. What the union of man and his world will be depends upon how he exercises his choices and how he constitutes himself and the world. Most existentialists are concerned with the ontic level of existing; how the individual actually makes himself and his meaning for his life on the actual level. Some existentialists are also concerned with the ontological level in which man's openness to Being is stressed. This level approaches Zen's noumenal cosmic consideration of reality.

The individual makes himself. Mankind is a project of man's own making. Human reality has been developed, created by man from his ground of existence which is always individual. Man has potential for developing himself and for determining the meaning, significance, and use of the world. Man does not have a fixed nature like everything tangible in the universe; not being completely bound by the same kind of natural causation, man is free to develop his own civilization and his culture. He learns to use language which enables him to pass on the human reality he has created to the next generation. Just as mankind has created human reality, each individual creates his own individual reality. He takes what he chooses from his society and from his own existence to make himself whatever he is to be.

Existentialism uses the phenomenological approach which centers on the human individual as the only witness to what appears as phenomena. One finds himself in the world at this "time" in history (this stage of the development of human reality) and at this stage in his own life. He becomes aware that his nature is different from things about him, that he alone has freedom to make of himself whatever he is to be, that he has thus far made himself through his freedom of choice. He takes responsibility for whatever he is, and whatever he is to be.

In authentic existence the individual examines all relational phenomena he encounters in his world and builds his own conscious structure which is uniquely representative of his own life-world. The truth for him is what he and he alone encounters; it is always subjective and relational, i.e., standing in relation to him.

Man has fallen prey to the objective world which he has fashioned and has become lax in taking full responsibility for himself. The objective world and its tangible beings are really "real." The nonsubstantial nature of man fails to compare favorably unless

12

it is vigorously activated. In man's fallen condition he is considered to exist in an inauthentic state. He does not accept his freedom and responsibility and exercise them in making himself. He merely goes along with the conventional way of life in which one does what he is supposed to do, what any well-adjusted social person would do under the circumstances. He recognizes only conventional meanings and values, and he uses all that is provided him by society to bring him satisfaction and to defend himself from anxiety. Anxiety does not awaken him as he immediately turns away from it to conventionally sanctioned activities and objects. He is a good consumer, a good worker, a proper family man, and supports the right institutions and organizations. He arranges his mind and his world in the usual way that the majority approves. With consensual validation that goes with thinking and doing like others, the inauthentic person accepts life as one of the masses and does not bother to dig deeply into his experience in search of quality. The inauthentic person seems to take the fruits of the civilization and his culture as his just due, and he takes little if any responsibility for adding to it. He actualizes himself in his work and in recreational activities in the conventional manner. His values are for preferred objects and patterns of activities which are the mode at the time. His emotions are largely stereotyped, his mental activities are predominately occupation with his everyday affairs in much the way that any other member of society would think about them.

Authentic existence is dependent upon the individual gaining insight into his true nature. Usually the individual is said to be awakened by anxiety, nothingness, or death. The person is shocked out of his everyday routine in which these serious problems of existence are smoothed over and covered up. If all that one can do and make of himself ends in death, does one give up in despair? One was thrown into the world without his consent, he is left here without any instructions, and in spite of his having been thrown, he does have possibilities and power to utilize them. He accepts his thrownness, and he assumes responsibility for his freedom and possibilities. He was thrown into the world with limitations, but he has the power to transcend. His limitations place contingencies on his freedom, but in transcending into the realm of possibilities

13

he can use his freedom to actualize himself. Recognizing that his existence is open to Being and Nothingness, his whole existence is opened up in a new way. He can now actualize himself in the light of Being rather than according to domination of the tangible beings of his world. He arises creatively in his experience which he differentiates into his own unique meanings and values. The quality of his life is changed.

Existentialism is largely humanistic; the individuality that it considers is the human aspect of man, and this aspect has been made within the socialization process. Since it has made itself it must take responsibility for what it is to become. It is the human aspect that has made itself which cries out for actualization, for a continual becoming. However, the gap between actualization and possibility is irreducible; and, hence, despair is ever threatening and guilt is always present.

The ego that one has gradually built up by his own efforts wants to be all that it can be. As Unamuno says, one craves immortality. This ego which has been carefully and painfully structured all one's life wants to be ultimate and to continue being ultimate, and, thus, to be immortal. One learned to talk, to be a human being, acquired knowledge of the world. One has made his ego as tangible as he can. It is a going concern, and one wants to keep it going.

Humanness of the personal ego is an achievement of man, alone. Reality produces the animal but not the man. It has been a slow hard struggle for man to develop his consciousness, language, and all else that is human, which is an unnecessary and unrequired aspect of the universe. The mind was developed in relating itself to the world which in turn is ordered by the mind. The infant human could not survive except that other humans take care of it. Thus man alone is his own project, all else is supported in nature. Man has created his culture by his own efforts, and it is only his self-created culture that makes him human. He has actualized his existence as man.

Man is open in awareness of being. His basic characteristic is care which insists that his attention be focused for his sake on being and reality. He could foresee his possibilities by transcending himself and all else, could choose, and could act with resolve to project himself in his own action. Thus, he and his world (the human world) were not produced by nature or reality, but by man in his freedom to actualize himself the way he has. He is not entirely free but faces a stubborn reality of substantive and factual nature which yields to man only according to its nature. Man studied this world independently of himself to discover its principles; he gained control of all he could and used it for his own purpose. The result is science which increases man's control.

Man is not fixed like other beings. He is always unfinished, always constituting himself in actuality through his own efforts. He is always becoming according to the way in which he actualizes himself. Man is not substance as other things which are constituted in space; he is nonsubstantial and time is central in his structure. He is a creature of the future and of his history, which is created in the openness of his possibility, as limited by facticity of reality.

This following review of Zen is only a brief introduction which emphasizes Zen as an approach to self-realization. Zen is a way of living which requires extensive practice; therefore, no written account can adequately provide understanding of its possibilities for self-realization. However, there is considerable Zen literature which is useful in pointing to the possibilities of Zen.

Essentially, Zen is seeing directly into Self. Self is not a separate being that one is; it is reality. No external agency of any kind, another person, literature, or any teachings can give a person realization. All is contingent upon a kind of self-discipline which will enable the individual to liberate himself from the dualistic conventional way of splitting reality into fragments which are only empty illusions of reality. Zazen is a method of meditation which enables the person to clear his mind of conventional thoughts and to reach his original state of oneness in reality. The basic idea is to gain control of the mind so all dualistic thoughts can be excluded and the original mind can be realized in its original clarity. This practice may vary in its results from realizing tranquility of mind to reaching satori.

In the usual sense there is nothing to learn; conceptual systems can only hinder; there is no achievement, in the usual sense, that can help, rather it is entirely the way of being, the being of the *is* that one actually *is*. One's reality is the same as all reality, and the

15

self and all other beings that one has dealt with are only hypothetical, serving only for routine activities in society. They cannot serve as a ground for one's existence.

With the liberation from dualistic thought the ego is eliminated, and all action comes directly from Self as expressions of Self, rather than being action based on selfish purpose of the ego. Human reality (ego in the individual) has been created by man, but it is not man. Man is being-in-reality, that reality behind what he has accomplished. Man is no product, not what he has made himself into, nor is the real world what he has made. Reality is one with man, and it is the living, breathing, thinking, and feeling man; it is not something he has done or something that he does. The true man leaves no trace, is not to be found. True reality is not to be found in any particular, yet it is because of it that particulars exist, just as it is because of man that human reality exists.

It is not the intent here to explain what Zen realization is; the purpose is to establish the fact that Zen depends upon realization for seeing directly into reality. Final success is called satori or enlightenment. Therefore, no one can tell anyone what self-realization is; for it can be experienced only beyond all that arises in experience.

Zen is so individual that it has stressed throughout its history that one must gain enlightenment for himself, yet it is so universal that one who is enlightened can tell immediately if another is enlightened. Zen sees the all in one and the one in all. It sees a complete identity in all opposites. Thus, the individual is the universal.

From the very first the task set the Zen student is to look beyond all phenomena that may become subject in the mind, that is, all that has its being in the world of consciously derived reality. In the teachings of Buddha, all phenomena are impermanent illusions which cover the "mind's-eye" to prevent one's seeing directly into reality. There are different means of achieving satori, but all practices have the purpose of taking attention from impermanent phenomena so that the eye of the mind may be directly open to reality itself. The purpose is seeing into Self, and Self is nothing other than the indivisible reality from which all impermanent phenomena spring, including oneself, and to which it returns. The Self is also referred to as the Void in which all has its "place." It can be visualized as the field in which all beings and events occur, the ground of being.

Language is designed to deal with the beings of the relative world, primarily with the impermanent phenomena which the Zen man must by-pass if he is to see directly into reality. Language designates the conventional meanings and values of the culture, which gives only a working view of reality. Zen does not propose to deny these conventional meanings and values but to recognize them for only what they are. This is illustrated by the Zen saying that when one starts to seek enlightenment, mountains are mountains and rivers are rivers. During the process of seeing directly into reality, they disappear as distinctions; however, after enlightenment they are again mountains and rivers. But after enlightenment they are more distinct, as they are seen not altogether in relation to each other, but also in their relation to the Void. This is roughly equivalent to saying that the conventional meanings and values are the most obvious view of reality before one starts to study Zen. One by-passes them, and goes to reality for its meanings and values in truth, and when the Self is seen into directly, nothing is visible to the Zen No-Mind but the totality of reality. But after reality has been clearly seen, the conventional meanings and values with which the language deals become clear for what they are. In Heidegger's view they stand clearly in the light of Being.

The view of reality of Zen satori transcends the realm of language kind of reality, but being all inclusive it comes back to language as to all other conventions. The impermanent phenomena which are our reality of ordinary life, of the relative and empirical world, are seen as samsara. Samsara is the world of phenomena which is seen as reality by the unenlightened. Nirvana is realized as the Void, Mind, or Self that exists behind all mental content. These are not two levels or aspects of reality after all, for reality is not divisible except in our dualistic minds. Nirvana is in samsara, and there is no difference. Ultimate reality is in the flowing of the impermanent phenomena of everyday life.

The most obvious course in the enlightenment of Zen is that

one liberates himself from the yoke of conventional meanings and values. These have been, for a lifetime, binding one to the extent that he is completely bound and can see reality in no other way. He is totally hypnotized or conditioned to respond in the conventional way of seeing himself in the world, in both action and thought. But when one succeeds in eliminating the conventional view, there is no other support for him but reality itself. Then one realizes that there is nothing really wrong with the conventional way of viewing reality; one transcends it, and it becomes as a tool for living in the world. Being outside the conventions rather than being bound by them, one is able to use them wisely in accordance with Reality or Being itself. One is then able to choose without particular biases that exist as long as one is bound within the conventions and blinded by them.

The whole universe is unfolding itself just as it should, and nothing that one can do upsets it. One can only upset himself. The body happens just like everything else; it works just like everything else. It comes into being and will pass away. Thoughts, feelings, and all differentiations of experience just happen as they happen. One has had enough freedom to create a petty self which he must now rid himself of. The berries are growing on the bushes, the leaves are beginning to thin out, the winds blow, the clouds appear in the sky. It all just happens, and nobody can stop it, nobody can distort it. Many fail to see it clearly and directly because of petty concerns. It is there just as it is there, and one is here just as one is here.

Zen says, work to get your food, eat your food, wash your dishes, and rest when you are tired. This maintains one's existence. Working for one's food keeps the body functional through the effort and activity. The food sustains the body. The rest refreshes the body, so the cycle of life can begin all over again. The mind is left free to respond to the ten thousand things in an amazement that is possible because it is indifferent to any particular as it focuses on the pattern. The aesthetic mind is beyond morals, there is no right or wrong, desirable or undesirable, nor any other opposite that it takes sides with. There is no affirmation nor negation. Phenomena arise as the individual is activated and they are relational to his actualization. The Zen man realizes instead of actualizes, and, therefore, the opposites do not exist as realities for him. He actualizes enough to keep properly activated for the expression of Being.

Zen would say, "Show me the man who made this human reality, show me the man who is behind the making of himself, and you will have the maker and not the made."

CHAPTER III

Identity

Identity is the age old problem of "know thyself." The self cannot be known in the sense that other things are known, it can be known only in direct experience. Identity is a process, and this is an attempt to indicate some of the possibilities of the nature of this process.

Identity as process can be understood in levels of advancement in inclusiveness as the individual moves through his life span. In the socialization process one comes to see himself as a conventionally defined individual. This is largely in the terms of individual differences as refined in differential psychology. Commonalities and differences are noted to determine the individual's unique constellation. The tendency is for the individual to attempt to objectify and make himself tangible. This focusing of attention in conceptualizations cuts one off from his intangible reality and results in alienation. Alienation is overcome by the individual opening himself up to realization of inner reality which must be self-validated. As the individual opens himself up to his inner reality he goes beyond individuality and discovers that inner reality is one and the same with outer reality. Thus, the individual goes beyond subjectivity in his inner realizations, and this is the same reality that is discovered outward, when one goes beyond objectivity. This is the "That art thou" of the *Upanishads*.

The most critical issue in individuality today is that of self-identity. To know thyself has always been recognized as extremely difficult, but it is widely held today that the problem of identity has become more acute than ever before. The individual has traditionally developed his identity through close connections in the family, community, and society. Now, he seems to be losing this relational identity in which he is known in a personal way. This relational identity is lost in the face of the anonymous crowd and the institutions whose bureaucratic methods demand a standardized, replaceable individual. In modern communication the whole world of the masses and their activities closes in on one to reduce his feeling of significance. Man is considered to be alienated from himself, nature, society, and God. The sense of a man standing in personal relationship with a personal God seems to be lost to most persons. The conventional concept of an individual who directs his own life, and who has significance in his world, has been greatly attenuated. The old concept of individuality will no longer suffice adequately for a convincing identity.

A conventional self-concept serves during the socialization period and perhaps as long as the individual is dominated by the conventional way of thinking, but with continual increase of insight into one's existence, the self-concept is too narrow to be significantly inclusive for the individual. At this state of personal development one must go directly to reality itself for his identity. Giving up his narrow concept of a separate self which maintains itself in opposition and cooperation with the environment (not-self), the boundaries are broken, and the individual realizes the boundless nature of self. He becomes an open process which has no definition and is centered in total interaction and interdependence in his life-field.

The emphases are shifted from the formulated aspect of life to the unformulated aspect of life, not that the unformulated aspect necessarily dominates, but it gains recognition and acceptance; this region of reality is opened up for the expansion into self-realization. The individual becomes a self-validating process with a corresponding process of dynamic identity.

Establishing identity is a process that is never completed, for life itself is never over, nor is there any boundary that definitely confines here-and-now existence. Definite limits do not contain the intangible aspect of life. One changes throughout the life span, and he must remain open in process of identity throughout his

21

entire life. The nature of man is to be eternally making himself and determining what he is, in fact and in mind. In thought and action, one is continually interpreting experience and integrating his interpretations into a total constellation. Each moment of continuous experience changes the constellation. And if one is alienated from his flowing experience, his identity is lost. It is impossible to know oneself once and for all, for one is never present once and for all.

No single particular conclusion will do; it is the total arising with the total, the total nonsubstantial with the total substantial, the directly realized and the actualized. But no fixed identity can be substantiated; the person and the world are both continually changing. Only as an object or a subject can one become fixed, and only through fixation can one stay with one object.

The search to "know thyself" proves difficult, for it has been implied in conventional thinking that one has some sort of substantial center which he can discover, if he looks close enough. A solid, tangible self is sought. One has not come to understand himself, because he has been looking for something other than his true self. Since self is not dense or solid, the individual is looking for something that is not there. His first elusive realization, before he attempted to compress the self, is the nearest that he ever gets, but he fails to realize this. The self is found in freedom and spontaneity, and it has the elusive quality which the individual hoped to condense into something definite; it is impossible for the individual to know self in the way he knows objects, for the self is not an object. The self is what is contemplating one's being as an object of some sort, and the self is not to become an object of this kind.

For the individual, there is always a kind of incompleteness. There is the subjective aspect of the individual which calls for an object for completion, an object with which to form a union. When the union with an object is formed, the individual is complete in this sense; that is, as complete as he will ever be. There is no one object which will complete him for long. As long as one lives he is ever seeking an object. In one sense, one's identity depends upon this process of forming union with the objective aspect of reality.

Alienation arises as a consequence of dualism being carried too far. At first man did not separate himself from nature. He later gained distance through the development of the mind; he made himself into subject and the world into object. He further separated the world into numerous independent objects; things were separated and viewed without their context. Man also viewed himself without context. Thus, extreme separation becomes unbearable in alienation, and the objective world becomes meaningless. Existentialism aims at reestablishing a tolerable relationship. The person is put back in his world, standing unified in relationship with things. Care and involvement have become central in describing man interwoven in his world. Heidegger's *Dasein* is man being out in his world inseparably united with it in care.

Meaninglessness is a symptom or perhaps it is central in alienation. Where there is meaning there is connection with reality and, hence, to this extent alienation is overcome. Values and meaning in this respect seem to be at the heart of human reality. There is no sense of reality when there is no meaning. Reality without meaning may not even be possible. A phenomenon becomes real to the extent that is meaningful. Thus, alienation nullifies reality. Meaning and values are central to the existence of the individual. Reality is whatever it means, and it is whatever it is worth. One might say that the connection of mind with that which is not mind is reality, both of them together, with each being only one aspect of reality which cannot exist without the other. This connection is made at the conceptual level in meaning and value, and alienation is failure to form this connection.

Alienation comes from ignorance which amounts to ignoring enough reality that even that which is not ignored is distorted in ignorance. Instead of the mind intervening to improve the relationship of one with reality, it disrupts it; this is the tragedy of building a kind of ego that is a disease. The desire to know may lead to closure which brings reduction in responsiveness. The necessary openness to reality may be closed too soon, or a closed pattern may develop. The ego tends to be a closure of this kind and it stands in the way of an adequate identity.

Individual reality changes throughout life. One source of being out of touch with reality, a means of self-deceit, is in trying to stabilize in an objective world. Not only is the world always dif-

23

ferent for each individual; it is different for the same individual as needs, satisfactions, values, and expectations continue to evolve.

It is of vital importance that we view individuality with all weaknesses, negative qualities, destructiveness, perverseness for sin, and limited response in the face of possibilities. To borrow Rogers' concept, there must be "unconditional positive regard" for man at his worst and at the heights of his glory. Above all, we cannot overlook the sordid side of human existence, the stream of cursed perverseness of man's history. Man resembles the devil as much as he does the gods, and this above all we must remember. If we take a too positive view of man, if we glorify him ideally, if we are not completely realistic in visualizing his reality, then the concrete individual that one actually is, and that one meets, may be condemned for defiling individuality. And, if we turn our backs on the failings of individuality in its concrete manifestation, our concept of individuality will be empty and meaningless. We will have forsaken existence for an idol, we will have lost our souls, thinking we could gain something more. Unless the worst in us is included, we cannot know our true identity.

The most dangerous error we can make is to repress or overlook one single phenomenon. It begins with judging. Thou shalt not judge. Thou shall not place desires for a particular above existence in the fullness of all it is. When we set up preferences which exclude any of life, we have doomed ourselves to ignorance. We cannot have it both ways, to know human existence and to have it like we want it. If we have it like we want it, we have removed ourselves from reality and cannot know ourselves. If we know ourselves we have given up our preferences which blinded us, in order to see existence and to know it.

Existence is a process and the goal of understanding it is to be identical with this process. This calls for a letting go of any fixed opinion of what one is. In letting go of one's identity one realizes directly in experience what he is; any afterthought one may have is only an abstraction and not adequate for identity. One is actually the seeing and doing power itself and not merely a result; one is a flowing process of power which activates itself in interacting with whatever it relates itself to, according to the nature of being and reality.

One may be closest to his identity when most puzzled as to his nature. One is concerned, stands poised, waiting to see what one is. One realizes that he does not have the answer regarding existence. The self can be defined in a negative way as emphasized in the *Upanishads*. One is not mistaking himself for any tangible aspect of himself which he can conceptualize. At such time one is more closely associated with that aspect of himself which is demanding an answer, than with any definitive answer which is available. One can act, and thus manifest himself, prove himself without having a verbal answer. One may arrive with the answer that he is ever in process, and that even this moment one is more his future than anything he has ever known or done. When one is uncertain and does not become desperate and defensive, he is open in all directions, in time and regions. When one is fulfilled by an object, he is closed to all else; he fulfills himself in the object. One has the best answer when he has no particular answer, but stands open in reality. This is the void to which one must ultimately come, and it is the final answer from the relative level: to transcend.

Any satisfactory identity one may establish for himself must be in relation to his whole being. Self-concept is obviously useful in as far as one can be known by conceptualization. Self-awareness can be extended to all that one experiences. Alienation and identity have been related in a manner that alienation interferes with identity. Alienation is produced primarily by the tendency to limit identity to a self-concept, so that subceived experiences are lost to identity. This has resulted in the individual being alienated from much of his essential reality, and since this reality he is alienated from prevents union with external reality, the individual is alienated not only from himself but from much external reality. He is left with only conceptual reality.

Man is both what he can realize nonconceptually and what he can actualize in thought and action. First of all, by identifying himself with his experience, man is convincingly what he can realize. This is the self-validity he establishes in experience. This is the ground of individuality from which the individual actualizes himself. All that man does and all that may happen to him must be accounted for in his identity. His possibilities for actualizing

25

himself must include the most dreadful thing which can happen to him, or that he may bring about. Death, disgrace, despair, sickness, and all that he can imagine, can arise as actual in his existence. On the other hand, his highest aspirations and the greatest joy may be actualized. But whatever is actualized, it is not once and for all, because actualization is a continual process, which never ends until something final happens to him. But anything final takes away existence instead of establishing identity. Death does not come to one as a final achievement. There is no final achievement in existence or in one's identity.

Actualization opens up into the lacking, open aspect of existence. Man is constantly at the crossroads (which in society is termed the modern predicament) of doing and not doing. His actualization depends as much on the options he does not take up, what would bring unwanted consequences, as on the options he acts upon. He would like to win the greatest prizes open to him, but, at the same time, he must avoid what will bring negative actualization. Identity on the actualization level alone is too uncertain to provide security. Identity in self-realization provides security; identity in actualization provides adventure and gain.

Identity is a matter of knowing who and what one is. In an important sense, the being is the knowing. As far as our identity is concerned, we are what we know ourselves to be. But if we do not know ourselves to be what we are in truth, then we do not have a valid view of ourselves, and we will not be satisfied with our identity. We cannot be self-validating unless we are open to our reality and the reality of ourselves. There is no self-validation on the conceptual level.

The main point in this consideration of identity is that the self-concept is inadequate if it does not allow for more than can be conceptualized. One has been led to believe, during his socialization, that he is, after all, only what he can lay on the line, make tangible and actualize. One is primarily what or who does this by which he is to be known. But this what or who is really nothing after all by comparison with all that is thought to be something. What one does and what one makes tangible take the attention from him and are misleading to himself and to others. The true source of identity is the mystery of Being. This is identity in self-realization. One actualizes himself in the way he stands out of Being, and this is identity in self-actualization.

The informalized side of self, the unformulated which consists of what might be called unconsciousness, feelings, attitudes, and intuitive impressions which can be only directly realized and not communicated or put in formalized verbalizations, must not be lost in one's identification. To omit this aspect of self would be giving up or letting slip by default the deepest aspect of existence and would alienate one from a major aspect of himself. Therefore, it seems vital for the individual to recognize and identify with this part of self and to be open to its activation. This self reality cannot be actualized, but it can determine the quality of experience and provide inspirations for actualization.

If we would claim our true identity, we must accept all reality. There is nothing wrong with reality; it is just what it is and nothing else. This means man and all the rest. Man has the power of mind and of action to create his own reality, but he is not to ignore the rest of reality. When he does this he is in bad faith, because he knows that his creation is dependent on him; it is a substitute reality. It does not contain the whole truth. Suzuki calls what man determines through his own efforts only half truth. Reality cannot possibly be other than what it is. We ourselves are reality and cannot be essentially other than what we are, no matter what we add to or subtract from it. As long as we are in bad faith, and know only facts that we have made to support the ego, we can never realize we are whole and perfect as we are. It is our picture of reality that is wrong, not reality itself. Reality cannot be wrong, all that is, is right. Man's picture of reality calls for taking sides and favoring some aspects of reality and disfavoring other aspects of reality, and in trying to change reality accordingly. And this, too, is reality, to be accepted. Man, until he gains insight, will go on distorting and disturbing reality, but with maturity he will know what he is and the kind of impression of reality he should have, a direct impression that lets reality be as it is.

In conclusion, individuality has been pushed to an extreme which brings alienation and loss of significance. Re-orientation of identity is required to include the boundless self, the nonsubstantiality of pure experience. This requires a shift from conceptualized knowledge of ego to include realization of the nonsubstantial self. The individual needs to be grounded in his universality in such a way that the universal force flows through his individuality. Thus, realization must balance off achievement to give actualization, conformity gives way to creativity, responsibility becomes primarily responsiveness, and leisure takes its place along with work. Meaning and value arise in the on-going process of life and are not frozen; there is no stopping the flow of life. Meanings are not to become conceptual forms which interfere with life.

CHAPTER IV

Self-validation

Self-validation of experience is of central importance in re-orientation of identity from the ego to experienced reality. It concerns that aspect of the experience that is established in direct meaning, as opposed to judging abstractions from experience. It has nothing to do with any external criterion of success, as reflected in making something tangible which can be validated by an external standard.

On the ego level, achievement which has conventional value helps to validate the ego. But for authentic realization, one's own judgment must be final. The self that is to be validated is not an ego at all; it is elusive, perfectly free spirit which exists without form, continuously with every particular form which appears. It is the self-validation of existence being what it is, in its own right, and under its own authority. It is like tasting food, the taste is just what it is, not a description of it to be validated in comparison with other descriptions.

Self-validation is final, and never contingent on anything except one's field of existence. One can be fully an individual to the extent that he places self-validation above all other validation. Consensual validation is important for conventional living, but ultimately salvation of individuality depends on self-validation. Too frequently consensual validation is gained by compromise of oneself, or it may even require outright pretense. In the end, nothing short of deep inner conviction will be satisfactory.

Self-realization is strictly personal, it is precisely what it is, and it is valid in itself. The self is lost if one considers unreal his inner (and outer) reality which he cannot make definite in a substantial way. One lives his realization: It is the ground in which he is embedded, and instead of dismissing it as of no value in ignorance, it should be considered of ultimate value. It is what the person is to himself, much more so than his measurements on attributes and his achievements. If one limits himself to what he can externally validate, he is only half a person, or less.

Self-validation cannot be obtained by deliberate effort to control; it is like the grace of God because it cannot be convincingly brought about. When one is convincingly in touch with his own being, he knows beyond any doubt. He is realizing validly when he is truly in touch with reality, he is reality, such as he is. Self-delusion is like bad faith. Bad faith is a lie but one believes it anyway. Self-validation is a matter of the deeper quality of experience.

Abstraction used in language is one means of conveying validation to oneself or to another. It cannot give validation. The abstractions can only communicate reports of validation. Self-validation is on the level of experience, and it does not consist in finding a proper abstraction which adequately represents the quality of this experience. Any validity that concerns communication is external to the reality of experience. If abstractions are used, all experience that does not fit the abstraction is lost. From habit in dualistic thinking, the great temptation is to start on the abstract level for validation and stay on that level; this is easy and calls for no reality except that of language usage, but there is no true validation for existence in this way of handling the problem. Forgetting that one is dealing with nothing but language, one may spare himself the trouble of verification in reality, under the false impression that reality exists in abstraction. This is the condition of alienation by intellectualization.

Self-validation is realization of existence, but explanation of this obvious fact leads to extreme difficulty of validation on the abstract level. One does not exist on the abstract level, and, hence, there is no true validation of existence in abstraction. This condition is reflected in the saying that he who is truly validated on the level of existence does not speak of it. He who does not know speaks up, but he who knows realizes that he cannot explain.

Abstractions have their own validity in abstractions, i.e., they must fit into the logic of the language by which the abstractions are made. The concrete particular, as in the case of one's own existence, cannot exist or be validated on the abstract level. But without some relationship between language and reality, language is of no use. Thus, its value varies greatly among individuals. If one cannot convey self-validation through language then language is of little use for that purpose. Abstractions and language serve the conventional level better than direct realization.

If one is more concerned with others thinking well of him than in thinking well of himself, he is thinking in terms of the wrong self. This "self" depends on external validation. Many have the notion that if others do not think well of an individual, he is not likely to have adequate self-esteem; this is a symptom of efforts to validate only a limited aspect of self. The value for self, in this case, is altogether on the ego level, which leads to competition and interpersonal dissension if validation is not adequate. Seeking self on this level is frequently a cause of exaggerated criticism of others, in which they are belittled or aggressively opposed. It is likely to cause one to cheat in bad faith, both in relations with oneself and others. It needs to be emphasized that self-validation is on the realization level. Instead of having to impress others or be accepted by them to feel his own worth, one first gains his own worth in his own judgment. Self-acceptance is basic to an appreciation of individuality. One comes to understand and appreciate individuality through his own experience in self-validation, and then he can fully appreciate others.

It is said in Zen that one must be evaluated by a master to see if he has real satori; however, satori depends on self-validation. The master does not validate, rather he seeks to witness self-validation. Only the self-validated can know self-validation. Not every person has reached the level of realization to be able to judge inner reality that is reflected externally. If there is an accepted master, then by all means one can be impressed by his opinion as to whether insight is present. But it is more difficult to validate a master than to validate oneself; one has firsthand realization. And this is a very important point. Does one personally know anyone who can fairly judge one's experience of self-realiza-

31

tion? And if one says no, is one being defensive or realistic? Who dares to pretend to understand the reality of one's uniqueness? Only the person himself can understand his own uniqueness, and he requires no external validation for his inner reality which is ultimate to him. Why should one depend on e__ernal evaluation of a master? There is no higher authority on the _ lgment of one's experience than his own, not among men. This is the attitude of the true individual.

The Zen master tests the student to evaluate progress toward self-realization. Before enlightenment the student keeps checking with the master to ascertain his progress, but after his enlightenment he is no longer dependent on the master's judgment. Suzuki gives authoritativeness of experience as one of the characteristics of satori. Many Zen stories concern the assertion of independence of an enlightened student toward the master. The student may speak sharply and even resort to blows. Suzuki describes an incident in which a student gave three blows to the ribs of one master and then sought out his original master and slapped him. The enlightened refuse even to bow to Buddha; there is a saying that if you see a Buddha spit on him. Another saying advises one to disrupt the *Sutra* rather than be disrupted by it.

There is no question but that I and I alone am right. But what am I right about? I am right about my own reality, and this alone. My reality is what it is, and I am realizing and making it what it is. But I am saying nothing about anything but myself and my "own" world. All things in my world are what I realize them to be, and there is no other source of determining meaning of them that is adequate for me personally.

The individual is the final authority as to the world in which he lives. Not that the individual always takes it upon himself to be deliberately and consciously such an authority. He may vest this authority for making himself and the world in whatever he chooses to vest it in. If he chooses a god, it is a god of his design or of his acceptance; if he lets science answer the question about the natural world or about himself, it is his decision that this view is used. If he seeks validation from others or from experimentation, this is his answer, and the responsibility for accepting the findings and conclusions is his alone.

What is at stake in one's own reality is that it appears convincingly authentic to him; he does not need scientific proof for authenticity. All he needs is faith that he is getting to his own essence. Perhaps as one is projected into the external world he does need external validation; he wants others to think that he is effective in his work and the public projects in which he engages. But only he can take responsibility for his inner existence. If one's self-validated reality is a psychosis that is all the reality there is for him. Fear of psychosis drives many people to the unending search for external validation, but that which can be externally validated is not self.

One is ultimate authority only in the region of his existence. Everything in the world has its own kind of authority, and it serves to keep the individual honest. In the individual's interpretation of the social region, it is a requirement that the individual deals with what is there and not with illusions or delusions of his own. Freedom and the exercise of one's authority depend upon proper recognition of the interdependency of all aspects of existence; one cannot deny or distort any part of his reality without distorting himself. His individuality consists in his being related to reality in one of its true forms, or in one of its true reflections if that is sufficient, as in the contact with only the afterglow of the sun in the sunset for an authentic aesthetic reality.

One can never be authentic as long as he is not prepared to stake his life on his own meaning and value, for what is real. One is doomed to be wrong, if he takes the word of another or the results of an experiment, for these conclusions apply to the situation from which they were abstracted. Buber says that truth in the world of man is not found in the content of knowledge, but only in human existence. Experience of existence is reality, but what is said of it can have no reality in itself. It may point to reality, not express reality. But any pointer is back toward reality which was there and is gone now. And while it is described, there is a new reality already coming into being, and more to come after that.

To expect other people to recognize one's authentic existence is to hinder self-validation. It is exactly by giving up all hope of validation by others, or anything outside oneself, that authentic existence becomes a possibility. A person may be looked upon as

33

a highly successful person but this seldom is because of his authentic existence; it usually is because of some product or result which may have little or nothing to do with the quality of his existence. He cannot gain authentic existence through the recognition of others, rather recognition will stand in his way, if he is impressed by the recognition enough for it to influence his opinion of himself.

Self-realization is complete in itself. To try to verbalize or otherwise express it to get it accepted or understood by others is extremely difficult. One may struggle for authentic expression and even if he fails it does not mean that his realization was not authentic. The failure can be in being able to make it appear realistic for others, and if it is truly individual, it may not be realistic for others; there is no one kind of individual reality that is individual reality for all. For example, satori cannot be understood except by those who have experienced it. Valid inner experience falls in the same category. The goal is not to make one's authenticity realistic to others, but only to oneself.

Frequently consensual validation may be a sign of failure to be oneself. Experience is known only in having the experience; therefore, one cannot expect another to understand any self-realization which is beyond the understanding of the observer. Consensual validation can be had only in common experience, i.e., the other person must have reached the same level of self-realization. To return to the extreme state of self-realization, satori, only one who has reached satori can provide any consensual validation for the experience. Obviously, to seek consensual validation widely leads to experiencing oneself in the conventional way.

If existence is to be truly meaningful it must be valid. Only the individual can sense its validity. Existence is continuous and self-validation must also be continuous. To the extent experience is valid it is significant. Significance then must be continuously present in experience, whatever form it takes. In going from one task to another, in eating one's food, in resting, in working, and in all that one does he must sense the quality of his experience. One has to be real to himself at each moment of his existence. One must answer without evasion all questions put to him by existence itself, as well as all in the universe which questions.

The authentic individual is not alienated from reality; he finds his existence is reality, and this existence is intrinsically valuable and does not depend upon results to give it value and meaning. One acts or fails to act according to his own understanding and sense of responsibility. Sensitivity to reality provides the cues upon which one acts; he is too wise to think that anyone could be a better judge of his existence than he, himself, is. If one is influenced by others it will be because he is considerate of them, not because he must be diverted from his course to gain their acceptance.

Self-validation rests on the assumption that self-realization is seeing directly into one's personal inner reality, without error. The eye sees the external object, and its seeing is validated in its agreement with other observations. One may need to make several observations before he is convinced of his seeing. So can the eye of the mind see the reality of the self and by repeated observations confirm its seeing. Action toward self-actualization helps correct one's realization. But action for results is of no use for the purpose of self-confirmation. Action for self-actualization is for self-expression to help determine the self and not for end results, except when end results verify the action. Testimonies of others who see their self-reality further confirm the assumption that self-validation is a possibility. Testimony is primarily of use not for checking the details to validate self-realization, phenomenon by phenomenon, but to validate the use of the method for each of us, to confirm the reasonableness of the method, or really, its validity. Testimonies validate the possibility of self-validation.

On the relative level, whatever the individual perceives and is able to integrate into his world, and which takes a place in his world and supports his world order, is his reality. This is the ultimate test of what individual reality is, on this level, and there does not have to be any external criterion for its validation. But stability is dynamic. Reality, for the individual, has its flowing aspect. Many things that are real now, may be real only temporarily. All phenomena are impermanent. If all phenomena are impermanent as Buddha said, then all psychic phenomena (though temporarily real) are impermanent, and mind only is permanently real. The individual is temporary as well as eternal, and he must live reality as manifested in both time and eternity. He is temporal through and through, but he is also eternal and universal through and through. What one was excited about yesterday has faded into his ground today; it is no longer so real, but this does not mean that it was nothing at all when it was dominant. This is a characteristic of our reality, part of it, that it comes and it goes. It is activated and it fades away. It ebbs and flows.

The individual alone can determine the meaning of his experience. He does not have to ascertain that this meaning is valid for all men at all times. It is valid only for his particular existence as he lives it, and if he is not to accept this as valid, then he gives up himself as the personal existence that he is. What is valid for one at this moment does not necessarily have any validity at any other time. One is not a substantial being that can be so validated. There is much that one moves among and interacts with which is clearly validated by others, but one's interaction with this objective aspect of his world can be validated by himself alone.

One's foremost responsibility as an individual is to express himself in congruence with his realization. All else must be secondary. One responds to the external particulars, but the external must not be the determinant (even though one recognizes total interdependence). The individual alone has the possibility of responsibility, the external does not. It is the self, and for the sake of the self that there is to be expression (actualization). The criterion for validation lies in realization and not in objective reality. One is a creature of Being, and his validity is of Being. Behavior is not self-actualization unless it is representative of inner reality; inner means within one's world and not encased in the body, it is realization. Outer in this sense all but disappears. The outer has no reality for self.

As long as one's truth is recognized as being only his truth, he does not have to fear that he may be a fake or a charlatan, for these terms are realistic only when one is trying to deceive others, in order to establish himself on the ego level. It is only when one is under the domination of socially introjected standards and ideals that he has any inclination to be other than what he is. Unless one is on the ego level working with categories of abstraction there are no means of deceiving oneself; it is only in taking abstractions from external sources that there is room for error. Error is made in forcing experience into borrowed abstractions to fit some external or introjected standard. Expected standards lead to distortion in favor of such standards. This deception of oneself is on the level of thought and action. Dishonesty with oneself cannot exist on the reality level; it must be on the level of differentiation and not on the level of being.

Most of the conflict between social conventions and individuality is created by the individual. He wants recognition for what society cannot possibly give him. The inner reality must always remain inner reality and cannot be projected permanently into any tangible form for which others may show recognition. It is up to the individual to solve this problem within himself, rather than project the problem into society and onto other people. His projecting this personal problem into society is the source of social discord in all who struggle nonconstructively against the conventions of society.

On the self level, the conventional notion that one can be judged by his peers is ridiculous. One has no peers. We are all peers in our essential reality, but there is no judging to be done on that level, because that is the ultimate in our reality. When it is said that we are to be judged by our peers the implication is that we are to be judged on the level of particulars where each of us is unique, with the only possible equality being our diversity. On the level of particulars there can be no more than different points of view, for each of us, and for each of us at a million times throughout life as circumstances within and without constantly change. From which reference point is one to judge and from which reference point is one to be judged? One is truly alone and without a peer to judge him, and he has no peer to judge. One must judge himself, but if he imposes upon another, he is to be judged. We come back to the conventional notion of being judged by peers. We are all equal in that we are not to be imposed upon, or we have a right to judge the imposer. This is in regard to external behavior and in overt particulars. Our discussion of self-validation is on the self level and regards covert behavior where one behaves for himself and his conception of the reality that he is responsive to and responsible for. One is to be judged in his overt behavior by all observers.

Revealed experience is the ultimate that we can know of our

reality. Objective agreements are only of abstractions. One's experience is his only reality, and only abstractions can be proven to others. Knowing that one's reality is beyond any external abstraction enables one to keep from confusing the two. Thus, there is no need to get one's reality mixed up with arguments over abstractions of what is said to be objectively true. Any expression or abstraction is only what it is when it issues from self, and then it is lost to the world of the ten thousand things. Only the self-validated can enter the gateless gate to self; for the externally validated there is no gate to self.

CHAPTER V

Self-realization and Self-actualization

The individual simultaneously exists in two modes: he is realized as potential being and he is actualized as a person. It is up to him to determine his identity through the balance he establishes in realization and actualization. Zen emphasizes self-realization, and Existentialism emphasizes self-actualization. Self-realization is related to self-knowledge and understanding; self-actualization is related to knowledge for control. For the ordinary person, conscious attention is focused upon the actual side and the realization side of existence remains largely unconscious.

Existentialism sees man starting in existence which is given; he makes himself and his meaning through his own effort. Existence is not subject to control. It functions as it does, mentally and physically, according to its own being. It is the ground within which one creates himself as an individual. Existence, being beyond control, is free in its functioning, and this freedom permits thought and action by which man develops his potentials. But his development of potentials must be in the world where there is opportunity, and as the individual makes himself he also creates his life-world. He is inseparably constituted in his world. Most existentialists take existence as the starting point and center their attention on the individual that is created on the relative level. The given existence is seen as potential, and their concern is with the development of these potentials. Man has freedom which enables him to make choices and take action for the development of his projects. He faces limitations and suffers setbacks in his efforts

39

in his self-actualization. Constant encounter with frustration is reflected in the amount of attention that existentialists give to guilt, anxiety, despair, and death. Thus, existentialism takes an extreme stand on the side of the individual taking full responsibility for creating himself as an individual. He develops himself in light of his existence and not in terms of conventional achievement. What the existentialists call authentic existence, we are calling self-actualization. Man's existence, the self-functioning being as potential, is understood through self-realization.

We have seen how Zen places its emphases on Being which it usually refers to as Reality. The individual as self is the ultimate in reality, and if man will not push too much for his own preference in making himself what he wants to be, he can appreciate the being which he already is. He is lacking in no way, for he is reality itself and not a unit which must carve itself out of anything whatsoever. The best thing that man can do is to let the human project take care of itself; it is impermanent, it arises out of Reality like a wave rises on the water. Human existence has no significance in its own right, all the learning and knowledge as well as all of man's achievements amount to no more than a speck of dust in the universe. Man makes his own anxiety, sorrow, despair, trials, and tribulations from his vain attempt to build a structure more impressive than that which is provided by Reality. But man is capable of realizing himself, not by active effort but by being receptive, and letting No-Mind (the reality within) do the work in its leisurely way. Suzuki equates satori with understanding and enlightenment; Kapleau calls it self-realization. The self to be realized is our reality.

What the Westerner usually overlooks is that in Zen actualization is always present for contrast with realization. There is always action in inaction. However, Zen action as seen through the view of the overactive Westerner seems rather passive. The ultimate in realization is seen in the most insignificant actualized particulars: a tea ceremony, a dried up dirt scraper, or a bare rock in a sand garden is adequate for revelation of the whole of reality. Realization is highlighted by contrast with actualization. Zen places nirvana directly in samsara, the particulars and the differentiations are always present, except at that stage in seeking enlightenment when the particulars are seen negatively. Then anything that can be named or pointed to is not self. But with enlightenment all of the particulars again fill the void in teeming activity. Zen does not insist on any specific particular, and anything actualized will do to reveal Self. Existentialism reverses this in having the actualized as the end; they would reach Being through effort. Zen would act because Being is present from the very first.

Each of these approaches is considering the whole man and, if properly understood and practiced, will bring both self-realization and self-actualization. Each of these systems stretches itself to do just this, but the focal points of effectiveness (in clarity) are as I have indicated. Existentialism demands actualization of individuality in light of Being, Zen demands that one take his place in Reality through realization. However, existentialism never really escapes the bonds of human reality, the whole world as we know it, must be limited to what man makes of it, if not in action, then in thought. Zen says that man cannot do or make anything of the slightest significance, whatsoever. The spirit of Zen is to act not for personal gain but for understanding and realization. And the spirit of Zen definitely demands no special effort which might interfere with the workings of Reality. Man cannot change reality in any essential way. The freedom of Zen has nothing to do with the relative level of actualization. The freedom of existentialism always has its eyes on limitations and situations, on the relative level.

Both Zen and Existentialism insist that if we would understand our reality we must go directly to our own experience. We must be able to differentiate between understanding and knowledge, or in knowing directly and in knowing about. All that is learned from the various disciplines, from all external sources, is only knowing about reality. Reality itself can be known only by experiencing it, one is reality. The knowledge obtained from external sources may be of incalculable help or harm. If it closes off direct experience or causes distortion it hinders the search for reality. If it can be used to help find clarity or what is realized directly, it will help.

Bronowski explains that man's identity is not by a special arrangement of the tangible aspects of a man but a self which is more than the sum of its parts. He discusses two modes of knowledge. One is the formalized mode which is gotten by observation and is the kind of knowledge used in science. The other mode of knowledge cannot be formalized; it is knowledge of the self which constantly grows and changes with experience. The self is that aspect of man that grows from experience and knowledge of it cannot be formalized. The total sense impressions, stored reflections, and the interplay of thought and action between them constitute a mode of knowledge that cannot be communicated directly through language content. This knowledge which cannot be formalized comes from experience and is fed back into experience and its accumulation constitutes self. This knowledge is characterized by a suspension of judgment and from it is knowledge of how to be rather than how to act. He concludes that the self cannot be formulated because it is perpetually open.

Aldous Huxley uses "understanding" instead of unformulated knowledge and "knowledge" for formulated knowledge. He is referring to the same two approaches to reality that Bronowski uses. Understanding is not conceptual and cannot be passed on. It comes when we liberate ourselves from conventional formulations and make direct, unmediated contact with the new, the mystery, moment by moment aspect of our existence. It is given at every level of experience, in perception, emotions, thoughts, in states of unstructured awareness, and in relationships with things and persons. Huxley thought that knowledge interferes with understanding which leads to self-realization. This is in agreement with the Zen practice of bypassing all knowledge in order to open the mind in realization. Knowledge can be added to at will, but understanding comes only if the old conditioning is replaced with a new unmediated relationship with reality.

In a similar way, Northrop uses two kinds of knowledge: theoretical knowledge is scientifically verifiable, and aesthetic knowledge is immediately apprehensible. He holds that complete knowledge requires a synthesis of the two. Our use of realization is in terms of Bronowski's self-knowledge, Huxley's understanding, and Northrop's aesthetic knowledge.

Self-realization is of the unformulated aspect of existence which cannot be made tangible, whereas actualization is known in terms of being actually brought about, as the formulated aspect of reality which is tangible, substantial, and verifiable in an objective sense. Realization is seeing directly into reality, or in letting reality reveal itself as it is. Actualization, in the broad sense, is any overt behavior or its conceptual representation. It is the way existence is actualized; it includes all that is done. In this respect it is action and achievement and any result or product that is attained. In actualization one works to make himself whatever he is to be in the world of affairs, as a person in society.

Realization is what is realized in understanding and self-knowledge. It is revealed directly without differentiation. Actualization is what is actually there in form and in conceptual knowledge. Both aspects of experience go on continuously regardless of particular action. There can be no moment in which we are not actualized in some form, nor is there ever the actual without realization beyond the aspect of experience which is actual and formulated. This realization of self has no form, structure, or substance. The actualized is subject to control in action or in knowledge; but the formless, only realized, is free and not subject to deliberation. The actual aspect of experience, events, situations, and objects, we can make clear and concise. It takes place in knowledge. The formless side of experience can be only directly realized in experience as activated; it cannot be clarified and made into conceptual knowledge.

Here we are recognizing two levels or realms of reality: the formulated and the unformulated, finite and infinite, tangible and intangible. There is the realm of Being, and there is the realm of beings. There is the realm of no-form, and there is the realm of form. Self-realization is identity with one's nonsubstantial realm of reality, and self-actualization is identity on the level of particular form. Self-actualization is the particular level as seen from the level of realization. In self-actualization the impossible task of making self actual and substantial is recognized, but the person so acts as to do the best he can to be worthy of Self.

Because of limitations, conceptual and actual, it is of vital importance that distinction be made between the realization and actualization of self. Otherwise, confusion arises because one cannot actualize what is only to be realized. For the realized, validity in actualization cannot be expected. Since realization, what can be

43

realized in the mind and heart of man, is on a different plane, and must remain on that plane, it does not lose its validity because it cannot be made actual. It is always obvious to the enlightened that the world of actuality and the world of realization are two different realms. Two errors can be made here: one is to see the oneness of existence dominated either by no-form or form, and the other is to see the particular forms without the oneness of all. Realization and actualization are two realms in self just as self and not-self are two distinctions made in dualistic thought. On the actual level there is differentiation and things differentiated, but on the realized level, beyond the actual, there is no differentiation.

Self-actualization is action grounded in self. Realization must be present in action if self is there in an enlightened way, for self is subject only to realization, having no form of its own. Then, self-actualization can apply only to action which reveals self to self. Self-actualization is effort for the purpose of revealing self. This does not mean as a personal or private self, for self is above and beyond any particular that is actualized. Actualization of self means that reality is activated, and that self is "place" for all that is made distinct, but self is not attached to anything. Self-realization is direct revelation of reality without consideration of action; it is Being independent of the form in which it is being. In the leisure state of mind it takes no form. In realization it takes no form. Only in self-actualization is it associated with form.

Depersonalization is frequently associated with alienation and in this relationship it is considered to be negative. It indicates that a person is of little importance. It strips the ego (the separate and distinct person that seeks a favored position in reality) of its significance. Depersonalization is thus the first step in enlightenment. Seen another way this depersonalization is actually a personalization of the universe; by the time the process is completed the personal has become universal, and there is no trace of the primitive personal pettiness. A person goes to the Zen master with the desire to be a super-person. He thinks he has gone as far in developing himself as he can go without Zen. Zen appeals to him; therefore, he will practice Zen to become a super-person. The Zen master leads him step by step in this process of depersonalizing himself or in personalizing the world. It can be seen either way, for in the end, there is no petty self to be concerned with. All of reality, in whatever particular it presents itself, now has self-involvement, i.e., the same personal concern that one had in beginning for his own petty self and its involvements. He is no longer a person but a reality, and none of his personal quality has been lost, only expanded.

A vital question for the individual is how full credit can be given to existence and its significance for man, in a world of things in which all the credit is given to obvious surface things and events. It is the depth of man and not the surface that is essentially man. Beauty is only skin deep, it has been said, but only the outward appearance shows. There can be no true beauty in outward appearance. How can one act sincerely when he realizes that all he can do is to show the surface that has little if anything to do with reality. This must be recognized or one acts in blindness, but how does one go on and act with vital significance in light of this? How does one perform this act in the light of reality to truly reflect reality? The answer might be that the significance is within the act and is not produced as result.

Self stands in the light of Being and the individual stands in the light of self. First there is Being, it manifests itself in self, and self manifests itself in the individual. But Being never becomes self, and self never becomes individual. The nature of Being is such that it provides the unformulated nature of self and self provides the a priori structure of the particular individual. Up to the point of the a priori structure of the particular individual universality exists. It is beyond the level of self that self-formations occur. The individual is self-made in the light of self; he is making himself in the arena of the world in which other individual beings are self-making themselves. On this level there is interaction and there is no absolute freedom in self-making of individuals. Individual beings become unique because each has a unique "place" in which its self-forming is activated. Each "place" has its "place" in ultimate "place." According to Nishida "place" is ultimate. To him "place" is equivalent to Zen Void.

Expression in the light of realized potential is a core problem of self-actualization. Expression must be congruent with self, and the results must be valid in external actuality. The purpose of expression is fulfillment of self and not satisfying external demands or gaining personal advantage. External demands and personal gains serve the conventional ego and strengthen it, and the ego activities and concerns interfere with and may almost completely replace self-actualization. Therefore, actualization requires that the realized potential be the source of the motive of expression and that the results be used to confirm the action and not the self. The danger is of self being forgotten in meeting external criteria of success. The goal of self-actualization is sufficient activation of self, and the resulting ego development and achievement are helpful secondary gains useful for living within conventional society.

Self is field of existence which is realized in experience. From the ground of experience all actualizations arise in differentiation according to meanings and values. What arises as apparently separate entities represents only a small portion of realized experience. The actualized is figure within the realized ground. Realization represents the ground of experience which is beyond whatever is actualized. Realization and actualization are two aspects of reality which we establish according to the direction of our attention and action. We can open our attention to that which is beyond actualization, or we can focus our attention on some differentiated aspect such as event, object, or abstraction. We can open our attention to awareness of totality of experience, or we can focus it as desired in deliberation. Furthermore, we can have a balance in a reciprocal relationship of attention in realization and actualization.

It is to be emphasized that self-realization is of reality beyond self-actualization. Self-actualization is through one's individuality; self-realization is of the boundless self beyond. Therefore, there must be the actualized individual to provide form for the formless self. It is in the interplay of the opposites that the extremes are highlighted. Thus, in contrast with actualization, where self is focused into structure, is the self as realized most vivid. The oneness of reality is seen only in contrast with the many; pure experience is seen only as the ground of the particular thought or judgment that exists within it, and arises from it. Reality as we know it is the interplay of the opposites, and the more this interplay is sensed the more vivid is our reality.

CHAPTER VI

Responsiveness and Responsibility

Self-realization and self-actualization are clearly reflected in responsiveness and responsibility. Pure responsiveness in which there is no effort to distort the reality that appears, in which nothing deliberate or voluntary whatsoever is done, is a necessary condition for maximum realization. Pure responsibility in which full and total control is exercised is the extreme in actualization. Through one's actions reality is activated in actuality, but in realization reality activates itself without interference.

Responsiveness is stressed here because we are taught in the conventions to be overactive and to distort reality in the direction of the values of human reality. We are taught that we must make things like we want them, that they are by nature wrong. We are wrong in our true reality, we are sinners. We must bring ourselves in line with proven external specifications. That these external specifications have never really worked, we are to congenially overlook. We are urged to be responsible, but we are seldom if ever reminded that responsiveness to reality is a necessary background to responsibility. There can be no true responsibility unless there is understanding that comes from responsiveness. We are constantly in interaction, and this interaction is carried out primarily through responsiveness and responsibility. Responsiveness rests in inner freedom beyond tangibles, and responsibility rests in freedom on the relative level within the limitations of tangible reality.

Responsiveness in realization extends beyond thought, conceptualization, or any form of intellectualization. It is of self-activated reality, and this activation is of united reality before any form of differentiation, such as of self and not-self. The activated is not self in the usual sense; it is realized through the loss of the usual self. It is beyond consciousness of a self. It is pure consciousness, free and without being restricted by detectable form; it is no-form, unformulated, flowing and self-determining. Any attempt to grasp reality at this level and take personal responsibility for it must fail. It must remain free and elusive.

Responsiveness refers to the level of realization and is not to be confused with perceptiveness on the particular level, on the level where everyday conventions are considered. It is in openness of the intuitive mind in direct attention to reality. It is in attention to the ground and not to the particulars which interplay on the relative level. It is in wisdom which is the ground of knowledge.

Supreme wisdom is beyond knowledge. It is freedom of the No-Mind. It cannot be thought. Nothing whatsoever can be done with it, for it is eternally self-determining. It is mystery, light, interplay between form, standing beyond form in the totality. Our ultimate source is pure attention to pure experience, and they are identical. All that arises, arises freely and is not to be grasped, not to be confined, nor is attention to be trapped. Attention is the one common thing in all thought, feeling and action; it is the one thing that cannot be denied if there is to be anything at all. There is a Zen anecdote in which a master was asked to write some maxims of high wisdom. He wrote the one word, "Attention." He was pushed to write something more important, and he wrote, "Attention, Attention." When told that there did not seem to be much depth and subtlety in what he had written, Ikkyou, the master, wrote the word three times. The man who had made the request became irritated and asked, "What does attention mean?" Ikkyou replied, "Attention means attention."

Being beyond control wisdom is of no practical use, whatsoever. Its mystery is realized in receptiveness and leisure. Identification with or attention to conceptual reason and values stands in the way of wisdom. Full identity with Being shifts the purpose to purposeless behavior. One does not try to exercise control, reality

48

appears to the mind. One has roots in Being to which he must open himself completely, if he is to realize wisdom on the supreme level, which is, of course, in all things. However, it is not the things, themselves, but in the ground and the being of all things. Realization of wisdom requires freedom from knowledge, but it permits freedom to work toward conceptualization and knowledge in the actualization sense, from within out. The highest living is not in attachment to the conceptual world nor to conceptual things of the world. All things are to receive full attention as necessary in maintaining life, but attention must be freely activated beyond deliberation. People usually assign their highest value to "things" and are concerned with their own petty selves and their own affairs. Most have not opened their minds beyond the confines of conceptual reality and its knowledge. For this there is need for compassion.

Responsiveness or receptiveness of the mind to reality beyond formalized conceptualization, in pure experience is continuous and free; reality on this level cannot be managed or controlled in any way. Here is only realization, and it cannot be brought into the mind for communication in verbalization. It is increased with the power of responsiveness, and it is the supporting ground of conceptualizations. It can provide no usable knowledge, and knowledge cannot lead to it. Only by responsiveness in realization is the ground of experience realized. It is experience that remains when knowledge has been extracted. Knowledge of experience comes from whatever can be differentiated and brought into abstraction. In responsiveness the source of experience is reached, and from this source all arises.

Man in his responsiveness is able to understand. In his understanding he can learn to exercise control. He makes himself human; therefore, he is responsible for all that he has added to and taken from this universe. Only he has freedom, motility, and can, in thinking and acting, determine his world. The world works in its own way and would determine man's world for him, but he enters into it and moves with or against it so as to effect the outcome. The individual in his responsiveness is open to Being which he lets be, but he takes responsibility for creating his own human reality, that which the world does not and cannot make for him. It is at this level of responsibility that the particular man is made, responsiveness opens into universality.

The petty self, the secondary ego, or the person as deliberately acting and using language, is our responsibility for it is created by our decision-action. The original self, the boundless self, is a direct manifestation of Being, and it is at the source of the petty self. It is the particular way that one is here that he is responsible for. For control of this particular person that one is, he has the possibility of responsibility; he can do this or that at each moment, or can he? This is the possibility in which one feels himself being responsible or irresponsible. One is responsible for making obligations and meeting them, for obtaining knowledge and using it, for what one takes from the world or adds to it, and one is responsible for whatever meaning all of this has for him.

Responsibility requires responsiveness to that for which there is to be responsibility. Responsiveness is in freedom, and only the free can be responsible. There is no freedom apart from reality; reality cannot be escaped, it can be distorted. The entanglements from distortion make freedom questionable; true freedom is reality. Reality is not something we exist in like a bird exists in a cage; the only conceptual reality we as humans know is the unification of the mind with its object, and conceptualized reality is like a cage. Both the mind and the object are caught. A free mind relates directly to reality and knows no cage. One has responsibility for seeing that neither the mind nor the object is caught. The mind and the object are united in free interplay.

Creative living is dependent upon receptiveness in experience to what is present and flexibility in responding in nonconforming ways with initiative and appropriateness. This is a state of openness and acceptance to what is present, both in totality and in the differentiations of one's world and oneself, and decisive action is taken with responsibility. Being open to one's world means not occasionally, but it means constant alertness in receptiveness to reality and in suitability of one's action. Creative living demands nothing less than continuous responsiveness as a basis of assuming continuous responsibility for one's actualization.

To exceed or to expect to exceed one's responsibility is painful and useless, and it distorts Being and reality by depressing receptiveness to it. One is responsible for letting Being be, but one must also give it the nonsubstantial attention that one needs for his own security. Aggression will distort it. Realization is guided by responsible responsiveness. Actualization is guided by responsive responsibility. Realization is of being, actualization is toward the world of particulars. Both have their origin in self. Responsiveness and responsibility are constantly in interaction and not to be separated. Both are required concurrently. We cannot be merely responsive. We must take responsibility for a suitable response in relating ourselves to the rest of reality. Responsiveness is reception of the given, responsibility is for our thought and action. One is as responsive to his own urges and inclinations, but no more, as he is to the rest of reality. Actually, there is no clear line of demarcation such that one may say that this force emerges from him and that one is external to him. As the Eastern seer looks within he sees no distinction in the inner and outer. The outer also comes within the range of realization.

All differentiated aspects of reality are in constant interaction, and the individual's inclusion in this interaction is through responsiveness and responsibility. In responsiveness other aspects of reality play upon him and in his active responsibility he plays upon it, and in responsiveness, feedback permits corrected action for more valid responsibility. Within the realm of existence there is continual exchange in the interaction of all aspects of reality, transaction is constant. One inhales and exhales, eats and eliminates. There is similar relationship between mind and objects of the world, between tangibles and intangibles. All about one is interaction, plants interacting with the soil and with air, also with light and darkness, and light interacting with darkness even in broad daylight to form shadows. It appears that nothing can be considered independent, that all that appears, appears in interdependence with all else. Therefore, responsiveness is in receptiveness and responsibility is in the interpenetrating activeness that is basic to the interaction of reality for the individual.

All individual manifestations are interdependent, but man can conceptualize himself as being independent. In his own mind, he can establish himself to a great extent as an independent unit. He has the capacity to make the illusion of independence seem real

51

to himself. This defies reality, as all is in constant interaction. Man's supposed separation from anything whatsoever is a curse, not a blessing. Openness permits interaction. The truth of interaction demands full recognition of interdependence. To separate oneself from part of reality to establish a separate and independent individuality brings alienation. This violates reality. One is all, and all is one, in absolute interdependence. All men and all of reality in the universe are interdependent, and man must recognize this and remain in open relation with all else, and he must be in constant commerce with it. Man is not real without the world, and the world is not real without man. Humanism or any other subjectivism is unreal when separated from nonhuman reality. Mind is one aspect of reality; mind is activated with the nonhuman aspect of reality.

As one grows in understanding, attention is focused more and more on the interdependency of all things. It is indeed fortunate for the individual that many of his ego ambitions are unobtainable. If they were obtainable he would then succeed in establishing himself in independence on the relative level. One would lose his interdependency with the results of severe distortion of his reality. Values must not be for things in themselves, but for all things in their place. Only so much good can come from any one thing, and that good can come only if the thing is kept in its place. All things are in their place and that provides their true meaning and value. It is an illusion that good can come from anything in excess or out of place, that anything can be independently determined. For example, the good of food, is food in its proper amount and at a reasonable time (place), and the same goes for all else—thinking, feeling, sensing, meditation, or abstracting depends on its proper place in the interdependent constellation of existence.

One is absolutely interdependent, not independent, not dependent. The secret of the balance and the meaning of existence is contingent upon interdependence, and to the extent it is upset despair, anxiety, and other kinds of dissatisfaction will be experienced. Reality requires proper transaction of interdependent forces in the life-field. The right kind of action sustains one, with concomitant satisfaction. The wrong kind of action or too little or too much upsets the balance. What one must do depends on the needs in interaction, and satisfactory interaction is the highest pleasure and the highest good. The pleasure derived from excess of any kind is an illusion. One's balance is assured by caring more for the proper interaction than for any specific particular. Anything that is wrong is indicative of the improper balance of things in their interdependence. What is right is indicative of proper balance. Every thought and act is to maintain this balance, and the balance must be understood to take preference over all else.

A person is his interdependence at the point in which all dimensions cross. This is his abstract definition. Concretely he is whatever his realization of this is. He is not this force nor that force, this desire nor that desire, this act nor that act, not this project nor that project. He is not the internal, the external, the past, the future, the intellect, the emotion, nor is he a sum total of all this. He is what is established by interaction; he is the transactional sum total. Anything that can be named about the individual is dependent, and all that can be added up is dependent, because the entire unit of the individual is dependent on a greater unit. All units open up into totality. All things have their place in the one totality, and they are to be realized in terms of their interaction with each other and the total. The heart can be defined only in relationship to the total body, the body in relationship to its physical world, and the mind in relationship to the intelligible world.

The mind and hence man's reality is most characteristically an interplay of nonsubstantial forces. To the one who does not understand this, it is nothingness. It is the void in which all tangibles happen. In the void the interplay of the opposites is the creation: To be and not to be, time and eternity, finite and infinite, good and bad, pleasure and pain, joy and sorrow, and action and nonaction.

Freedom permits the interflow of forces, in their interplay. The individual is free when identified in this manner. Reality is uniquely different for each individual; each person is a system, a reality, a process unit of his own, and numerous such systems work freely in their inner interaction. This interaction process is the reality one recognizes himself to be when the separate ego is given up. He was this process all the time, but he thought himself to be either dependent or independent. The enlightened person who sees himself in this manner chooses to act freely and spontaneously without restrictions or conflicts. Here responsiveness and responsibility are unified and not separate as on the relative level. This is true understanding of individuality, for what is right for the individual is right for him alone. He is process with its own reality; i.e., he is the reality that the mind is open to, and there is no proper judgment that can be made by any other individual or from a public frame of reference. The reality of the self is self-creating; it is not something that must behave in an externally determined way, not on the ultimate level. There is no boundary between the individual's reality and total reality. Thus, the reality of the individual is reality. One is identical with reality.

Reality manifests itself in mind in the direction of man, it manifests itself in substance in the direction of the natural world. Human reality developed through the interaction of these two different kinds of manifestations. Mind is free, but when it develops itself into its conceptual structure and becomes representative of the relative world, it loses much of its freedom. The free mind is the original mind before differentiation; it is the Zen No-Mind, but to deal with substantial reality it has to give up part of its freedom, becoming dependent upon form which will represent substantial reality. When the union is made with mind and substance each is dependent upon the other, and they both exist in interdependence. As long as the mind works in representation of the external world it must have objective validation, but when it turns back to Being through itself there can be only inner validation. The mind works in interdependence with the world, and it works in interdependence with Being.

As we have been emphasizing, mind is free and because of this freedom man was able to develop human reality. Human reality is the interaction between the mind and the natural world. In this interaction the human ego is set against the non-human world. Human reality then is bound up with the tangible world, and man is not free except within limits. The variations in cultures reflect freedom as opposed to a structure that predetermines human reality. Beyond the ego is the boundless self, mind is free, for it is identical with reality. Man is partially free, being in an interdependent relationship with his world. Mind (as Zen No-Mind) transcends interdependence of man and his world. In responsiveness man can realize the original mind, and in exercising his responsibility he thinks and acts to make his interdependent place in the world.

Man as ego is in a way like a squalling infant; he is willful, and that is his beginning. He is helpless but still he makes demands. Out of his demands come his first feeble efforts. From his efforts come destruction and creation. This is central to human reality. It protests, it is not to be ignored. It demands its feeble way. Like an infant, it will destroy some of the things in its "room" before it learns to live with them and take care of them. Only in asserting itself vigorously will the infant discover himself and external reality and learn to live in reasonable harmony on the relative level, and then move beyond to greater harmony on both levels. Individuality is all but torn apart through man's determination to assert himself to the point of no longer being responsive to anything but his own results and ambitions. He will have his way before he discovers what the true Way is. Whenever he begins to awaken he finds himself with habits and conditions which bind him and from which he must liberate himself. However, individuality on the relative level must not be stifled and rounded off, it must be exaggerated to the point of expanding itself beyond the limits to the boundless self beyond. This is why external controls or limits cannot work to provide a society which de-emphasizes individual rights for greater social harmony. It is only through exercising relative freedom that man can through responsiveness to reality arrive in selfless reality beyond separateness.

Collective movements such as found in totalitarian countries must fail because of the strategic place of freedom in human reality. Individuals must have freedom to exercise their responsiveness and responsibility in interaction on the relative level before they can reach full maturity. The perfect society awaits the perfection of individuals who are convinced that reality will have its way; the perfect society cannot be established by collective control.

CHAPTER VII

Conformity and Creativity

The individual is essentially creative in spite of and also because of his need to conform and to meet external demands. Conformity and creativity are essentially complementary in nature, and their interaction gives each its meaning. Conformity taken alone is too routine and stifling for the human spirit, just as creativity taken alone does not provide enough stability for the freedom of the human spirit. Conformity is only form, and the heart of the matter is the projection of the human spirit into the form. Conformity is the cup which holds the tea, and the shape of the cup does not determine the taste of the tea.

Form must be occupied by the spirit, and the spirit must have a form to occupy. This is the simplest statement to be made about the interaction of conformity and creativity. All form is empty except for the spirit that lives in it. If the spirit is not projected into expression, the expression is empty and the spirit dries up. The individual and his activities house the spirit.

Free creative existence must have form, but no form is adequate for long. Creativity has its unending fate to continue throughout life seeking adequate form. This effort to find suitable form is associated with all that man has produced, all that he has added to this world. Such is the difficulty of finding expression that can do full justice to free creative reality. And this seeking suitable form never ends with any achievement. This is a lifelong process of birth struggle, being interpreted now as painful and again at another time as blissful. Life is creative, and this creativity is too strong for most to face unflinchingly; therefore, relief is sought through distractions with things which are by-products of it. Today's formulations serve only today and pass away. At each moment one is forever formulating new meaning, and meaning itself is a process not to be lost in its formations.

Creativity and nonconformity are by no means synonymous. If nonconformity is the purpose the individual ends up as much a slave to nonconformity as he would to conformity if it were the purpose. There is little virtue in being different for the sake of being different, or in change for the sake of change. Hasty change tends to bring even hastier change. Neither being different nor constantly changing will pass for long as quality or excellence beyond the customary. Both conforming and nonconforming put too much emphases on form. Form is empty except as it is filled with the quality of experience; therefore, form is to be seen primarily as a by-product on the one hand and as a mere tool on the other hand. If you would dig a hole would you use a stick instead of a shovel merely to avoid doing the conventional?

True individuality is not achieved by outer form alone; creativity is not dependent upon results. Creativity is beyond the particular forms used. It will not help one's creativity to grow a beard, dress differently, or even to think about different things. More than likely man has been preoccupied with the right things all along. No final answers have been found because answers are in activation and response. What occurs, appears, or is realized asks the questions. And life is never a question; it is the answer. Living is primarily listening to and answering the questions but answers are only for the moment, a passing answer that settles nothing at all. Life is nine-tenths listening and one-tenth action. Listening to the reality that is actually happening with full attention on all levels provides the questions of life.

Creative existence is alive, vivid, spontaneous, alert, and unique in its happening. Conformity is a routine, deliberate, formalized, and standardized pattern consisting primarily of habits. What is observed can usually be classified by what is done in conforming, but for the individual it depends on the approach and not what he does; that is, upon attitude and the manner in which he projects himself into his daily events. The tendency to determine con-

57

formity or creativity by what is done is a mistake. Living naturally and creatively may take, what is to an observer, an identical form as a routine life of conformity. For the observer with understanding and empathy the creative aspect of the life of another may be realized.

Conformity has to do with conventional form. Creativity has to do with free spirit seeking form. Conventional form is the accepted manner of expressing the culture within the social framework. The reality of the individual is of a free and creative nature to be expressed in available form, but there is always the possibility of creation of new form. As the individual expresses himself in society and in his personal life he is usually making some sort of coordination, and perhaps compromise, between the available form and his creative spirit, which is realized beyond conventional concepts. Concepts and language are conventional forms available for formalized thought. Conventional success depends on use of accepted available forms for conventional achievement. Individual success depends on the extent to which creative spirit is expressed.

To try to establish one's individuality by nonconformity does not carry one beyond the level of conformity. Individualization depends on appropriate interaction with reality and cannot be achieved through technique, knowledge, or form; therefore, to preoccupy oneself on this level will prevent growth. Conforming is definitely not the answer, but neither is nonconforming the answer. The answer is not to be found on this level. Zen does well in this respect. It shows no interest at all in conventions. It sets the task of seeing directly into reality and frankly admits that for the enlightened one outward behavior may not be changed. The enlightened takes up again in ordinary behavior, using the conventions freely but not depending on them to substantiate himself. All his behavior is beyond conventional meaning, whether it conforms or does not conform makes no difference to him.

The individual is subject to pressure to conform from two sources: The demands and expectations of the conventions of society and his own habits which form his own personal conventional way of living. A person can conform and minimize his individuality, or he can engage in creative interaction with both of these conventions. Creative interaction with these conventions will keep

58

them from crystalizing into binding forms which stifle creativity and limit freedom. Even if one is a slave to his habits, this does not mean that he cannot respond to them creatively in finding new meanings and values for them. The final meaning of a habit depends on its place in one's unique existence, and as aspects of existence change, the meaning of any habit changes. But if one is caught in conformity and makes no special effort, meaningless behavior gradually develops from following routines in a lifeless manner.

Unfortunately conformity to one's own personal conventions is called stability, or even integrity, and it is considered to be a virtue because it stabilizes the individual into the conventions so that others may easily conform to him as part of the conventions. The danger in this for the individual is obviously that the free creative process of existence is blocked and alienated from the self-process. Thus, in considering one's stability or integrity it becomes of vital importance as to the level with which one identifies. Identity with oneself as process gives stability in constant change and freedom, whereas identity with the particular level binds one to form in his search for stability.

Conformity and creativity interact to support each other. Conventions grow out of creativity (not conformity), are sustained by creativity, and are used as a base for further creation. Convention is like a base camp for an explorer. The explorer leaves the camp for his adventure and returns to it after his creative explorations. He may keep his camp in order with no changes, or he may change it daily, but essentially it remains the same base camp. It is with eager curiosity and earnest seeking that the explorer goes forth each morning; it is with thankfulness that he returns to his shelter for its comforts. The explorer uses all the proven conventional methods and tools available to him in his explorations; it is his discoveries that are new.

Interaction in society is necessary, but the nature of this interaction can be determined by the individual if he exercises his freedom and responsibility. If freedom and responsibility are not exercised society will determine the nature of the individual's interaction. Modern society intensifies the need for interaction, but increased leisure time gives additional opportunity for freedom.

The exercise of freedom and responsibility is also necessary if the individual is to use his leisure time to increase the creative nature of his existence. If the individual fails to exercise his freedom with responsibility in that part of his life which belongs to him, he will become a victim of escapism, inertia, and enslaving practices provided by the society. There is also a grave danger that he will conform to conventional recreation in a noncreative manner.

The conventional view of oneself is the self-concept. As we have seen in the chapter on identity, the self-concept is not adequate for the whole person. However, the self-concept is vital to one in his interaction with the conventions. It is important that one use all means provided by the conventions to understand how he is viewed and how he should view himself as he takes his place in society. The self-concept, like all other conventional forms, is to be vested with one's creative spirit. It is the form for the free self in its transactions with society and with others in the course of daily affairs. One can freely use the self-concept if he remembers that it is not adequate for the aspect of existence which is not focused into conventional activities.

One has the possibility of interpreting everything that happens to him and everything he does for a creative revision of meanings for himself. This possibility exists even in the most routine things. Each of these conventional situations and objects is unique when given creative meaning. When stereotyped and taken for granted they become flat. Going to work, morning after morning, may be merely going to work, but even this routine event is open into the realm of possibilities. There is that portion of the world through which one goes, the sky with whatever is happening there, the people behaving as they are and having their preoccupations, nature with all its happenings, and all of this is an indivisible aspect of the entire universe, opening up into history, culture, and society.

Not only can one find new meanings for the routine, through the conventions one is led to the culture. An example of this is the written language which has taken form through the creative efforts of our great writers in describing the reality they experienced. And by the individual's own creative efforts, he is able to reactivate this reality within his own experience. And as he assimilates in this creative manner the cultural reality he becomes in-

60

creasingly open in his own experience to his own self-reality. This creative process continues in his experience primarily in the form of realization and actualization. In realization he is receptive to his reality, and in actualization he strives to find ever more suitable form for its expression. This may bring about refinement of the conventional form, especially in meaning and value.

A fully responsible individual cannot overlook the fact that all that makes him human has come from the long and devoted efforts of the race of man. The whole human world as we know it today, including the cultural world and the social world, has been developed from scratch. If man had not devoted himself to this development we would still be living in caves if we could find one and were strong enough to drive out the animals and other men. We could not be speaking to each other, writing, reading, exchanging ideas, or obtaining food in neat packages unless man had applied himself creatively. In our human reality there is much truth, justice, individual rights, wisdom, and other intangibles which have evolved out of the experience of man. There has been much war, crime, suspicion, distrust, and other negative aspects of man which sometimes seem to dominate our judgment in considering the state of man. But all would be turmoil and uncivilized strife if our way of life had not been prepared for us. This is not to say that all is well. Too many men are still preying on others in more subtle ways than in past ages.

Social reforms are needed but until individuals develop to the point of creative responsibility, there can be no clear idea of what reforms are needed. Reforms based on the need of less than responsible persons will build a society that fits irresponsible individuals and will not be a society to further individualization, but one to accommodate rather than stimulate. The individual is responsible for the way he interacts with society, and society cannot assume responsibility for this interaction. It is a matter of how we develop individuals rather than how we develop society to accommodate individuals. The requirement is to move toward more freedom for individuals, but this cannot be achieved when it interferes with other individuals. Reforms to help special groups should not be at the expense of anyone else, a way must be found that helps each without taking from anyone else. The movement must be toward maximum freedom for the greatest number. Restrictions must be imposed on all who would interfere with the rights of any other person to be free. Only in this manner can society be improved for the individual. Except for rapid correction of obvious injustices social reform should be by evolution rather than revolution.

Conventionality and social stability are of vital necessity for individuality. It is incomprehensible to dream that the enlightened individual should seriously want to disrupt the order of his society. The freedom that is most valuable can be found only in order. Inner freedom requires external limitations. The external limitations are the boundary of the forms which create the containers for this precious freedom. There is no formless self without finite existence, just as one cannot have water unless one has a container in which to put it. In a similar way one cannot have freedom unless he has something in which to put it. Water for which one has no container is not his water, freedom for which one has no form is not his freedom. The water is the water and not the container. Freedom is the freedom and not the form; the form has absolutely no freedom. If man is defined as a form he is not free. Man is not primarily form. He merely utilizes form.

The forms by which things are done, the things which are made and used, the manners which govern social behavior, the events and situations together with their expected meaning and value, and all other forms of conventions are to become secondary, with the individual functioning without violating them or without finding himself restrained unnecessarily. This becomes possible only when the conventional form is no longer an end but a tool to be used for another end, for an end on a higher level of existence. Language is a convention that is necessary for expressing understanding beyond the level of language. Language does not exist for its own sake, but that it may be used in referring to something else. Just as the language can be used conventionally and creatively at the same time so can other conventional forms. If one would be understood he must use conventional forms, but if one has anything worth understanding it will have to be beyond the forms themselves.

Most people fight to be accepted and lost in the crowd, and

at the same time to stand out as an individual. This can be a source of great conflict. It is a conflict to the extent that one identifies with the social self or ego and depends too much for satisfaction on this level. But if one identifies more with the nonsubstantial self, then he has a constant and supporting existence when in the crowd. Competition and establishing oneself in the crowd is no more than a game which we play seriously, but which is not ultimately important. In fact, the playing of the game as expressing or actualizing ourselves is what is important, and the opposing players are necessary. Unless they try to keep us from winning it is no real game at all.

Until the individual transcends the forms of the conventions, even as he uses them, he will not be free to be the natural creative process that is his true reality. As long as he depends on the conventions to substantiate him his individuality is not free. He will be dominated, and his freedom will be stifled. To be free and creative in interaction with society a very delicate balance of interdependence is required. If there is a need to dominate, the conditions under which domination is possible will enslave. Likewise, to submit to dependence will enslave. A desire for independence will disrupt the free interplay of interdependence and cause an interfering drag. Independence is thought to be a virtue and is highly valued in our conventional thinking, but in reality nothing can be independent.

"Freedom from" is the beginning of freedom. It is liberation. And liberation is freedom from that which would contain. In the case of conformity it means a shift of motivation from that of being dominated by results and conventional ways of acting and thinking. After liberation from conceptualization, psychic energy flows into conceptualization without becoming a captive to it. "Freedom from" is the foundation of freedom; it permits pure responsiveness, whereas "freedom to" requires responsibility that may also bind in the exercise of freedom for a purpose. Zen prefers purposeless behavior, seeing it as the ultimate. As in Taoism behavior is the natural and inevitable outcome of one's freedom which is not given up for a particular result. "Freedom from" is the heart of realization, and "freedom to" is the heart of actualization. However, there is no real distinction to be made because freedom is the state which permits the activation of reality in self-determination.

In considering the span of life in relation to conformity and creativity, it is usually accepted that creativity is present in the spontaneous living of the child, but it is drawn into conventional thinking and acting through social reinforcement for approved behavior. And for the majority this socialization captures the creative spirit, and life becomes predominately conforming to conventional meanings and values. More than likely most individuals believe themselves to be much freer than they actually are. Only a few liberate themselves from conventional domination, to return to self-domination of the creative life-process. This going beyond the conventions is what existentialists refer to as authentic existence. It is self-actualization guided by self-validation. Zen sees the ultimate going beyond the conventionally dominated existence as satori, or enlightenment, in full responsiveness to reality.

A creative cycle seems to be present within the forms of nature. Spring follows winter by uniquely happening in its creative way. It always varies according to the interaction of all the forces involved. In man each event would follow in the same way if man did not emphasize the form, the routine, and tend to stereotype them. Thus, relationships between two people tend to become frozen into something like the psychoanalytic transference manner, instead of being free and spontaneous with each meeting. The individual's daily life, likewise, tends to become routine and dull, as he goes about life and work as usual. This routine view is an artificiality that man has imposed on his life-process for efficiency and achievement's sake. Thus, the creative flow of life is all too frequently seen as conformity to the things people find necessary and satisfying in light of their needs. They work routinely, eat routinely, and seek entertainment routinely. Creative living is lost. Creativity is a "lining" projected into form, that living quality that flows through each incident. It is always present, but attention is frequently diverted from it. Conformity is found in a tendency to observe reoccurring acts and events to be similar, but behavior like nature moves in cycles of ever renewal, day and night, winter and spring, and beginning and end. In conformity what is overlooked is the creative side of the cycles as only the routine aspect is observed.

The creative process of existence can best be seen as the free interaction of all forces of the life-field. Human existence starts with a mind that witnesses all that comes before it, and the mind continually takes the shape of whatever it deals with. It is representative of the reality that it witnesses. There can be no stopping of the mind or reality is lost, and one is alienated from it. The mind is to be free to enter conventional thought, engaging in it vigorously without being caught up in it. It freely takes the forms but does not become dominated by them.

Creativity on the relative level consists primarily of selection and arrangement through differentiation and integration of ideas, actions, materials, and other phenomena. Each builds his world in this creative manner, makes arrangements within his existence and through responsiveness and responsibility establishes balance in the constant interaction of the forces involved. For each his arrangement is always meaningful. Conventional meanings are better for the formalized side of reality, but the meanings for the unformalized will depend upon the individual. Manners are social traditions, and one is not to show originality in them. The way one feels and the private meaning he alone can provide are his responsibility. This is his individuality, what he himself provides as he is going through the form of life, the form of life meaning the particular activities that are appropriate for him to engage in.

True individuality is in existence beyond the conventional world and the conventional ego, where one actually becomes fully conscious of being an individual. One is born from the culture into reality itself. Exceptional individuals have been going beyond the conventions for centuries, but always man as truly individual has had to be born from his culture through his own efforts; he must suffer the labor pains as well as the birth pains. With understanding of his own unique collection of the forces of nature and of the culture the person moves beyond the conventional world into the world of reality. He cannot move into the world of reality by imitation. His individual world of reality must be of his own creation, rather his reality is self-creating. In as far as one's essential existence is concerned he is through with ultimate concern about the conventional world, but he goes about it with care, knowing that most individuals are still depending upon its stable structure.

CHAPTER VIII

Leisure and Work

Leisure provides opportunity for development of the self-realization mode of individuality. Work is more closely related to self-actualization. In leisure the informal side of private life is developed, with a minimum of pressure from external demands and expectations. In work the ego is actualized, the active and more tangible evidence of one's existence. In leisure one takes his existence as it is, being receptive and open to it. In work one makes his place in the world of affairs through highly structured activities which are usually predetermined. Leisure is an opportunity for one to contemplate his existence and speculate about further projects.

Work is associated with the substantial which can be analyzed, manipulated, and controlled. Leisure is associated with the nonsubstantial which is not convertible into tangibles and not subject to direct control or to external criteria. Work is concerned primarily with that side of reality which is man-made or discovered. Through work man cuts the tree and makes lumber of the timber and uses it for whatever end he has in mind, which is within range of its use. Through work man isolates intelligence as a mental function, shapes it up and further develops it, and uses it to whatever end he desires. From the world of mental phenomenon he develops principles which will work, creates norms, invents conceptualizations, and arranges them to serve his purpose.

Work tends to be result oriented. Work is for a practical purpose. The clearer the purpose and the clearer the knowledge of a detail plan for achieving the purpose the more effective the action.

66

Efficiency is gained by eliminating all useless efforts, by directing each effort as effectively toward the desired results as possible. The best model for work is a machine. The action of a machine is limited and confined to its functions; its structure prevents it making variations from its designed pattern. Efficiency in man is increased the more machine-like he becomes; all variations must be eliminated and the attention must be directed on the process for results. Many human qualities such as excitement, irritability, or reluctance will be likely to interfere. Attention in work is on the process for results, and much humanness is given up for the sake of the results to be obtained. The purpose in leisure is reversed; humanness is to be experienced and this experiencing is the purpose, and the end result is a by-product.

Work activities are externally controlled; this control may be the demands of a supervisor, the needs or demands of a client, or the form that must be submitted to for the required results. Work thus limits opportunity for expression and gives only a narrow range for self-actualization. The opportunity for self-actualization may vary from little in some work to a maximum in some professional or creative work which provides a wide range of freedom. Routine work gives a certain amount of mental freedom. The more routine it is the more automatic it can be done and the freer is the mind. Routine mental work does not have this free aspect. Work varies greatly in opportunity for self-expression, but most work provides more opportunity for self-actualization than is generally utilized. The utilization of work for self-actualization is greatly dependent upon a person's creative initiative. This is also true of using conventional forms creatively.

Pieper discusses leisure as the basis of culture. Leisure is a mental and spiritual attitude; it is not simply the result of external factors, it is not merely spare time, a holiday, a weekend or vacation. He describes it as an attitude of mind, a condition of the soul, and as such is the opposite of the ideal of work, which he analyzes as activity, toil, and social function. Compared with work as activity, leisure indicates an attitude of nonactivity, inward calm, and of silence which lets things happen. This silence, he states, is a prerequisite of the apprehension of reality; it is the soul's power to "answer" undisturbed reality. Leisure is a receptive

67

attitude in which one increases his apprehension of the totality of reality. It is an experience of serenity, recognition of the mysterious nature of the universe, deep confidence, and freedom.

Leisure is a state of being. It is a gift of existence, and it is the basis of understanding self, our primary experience. It belongs to the inner world, to the source of life within the person, and it does not end in result, not even when activity springs from leisure and ends in result. That which can be praised as achievement is secondary. Leisure is the source of true quality and excellence in individuality. Only a minority of individuals have developed their capacity to experience true leisure, but the potential is in all.

Gradually mistaken impressions come to us if we submit to be conditioned by things that are of the work category which arise in leisure and come to be confused with leisure. Leisure is to let things arise but not to take them up. Leisure belongs to the ground of being and not to specific objects or projects. A good example of how the leisure state is lost to the work attitude might be reading for no purpose other than leisure, but when one begins to recognize benefits that come from reading, one may plan a program of reading as a background of knowledge for achievement, and, thus, take reading from the realm of leisure to the realm of work.

Nirvana is pure leisure, samsara is work. Zen stresses purposeless living directly from the No-Mind; this is leisure. Suzuki emphasizes the requirement of no stopping of the mind in Zen. This is the leisure condition of No-Mind that lets all phenomena come to the mind freely and leave freely, with the mind taking nothing up to hold on to. This is analogous with the impermanent working of samsara in the void, the mind as the void and the impermanent thoughts and ideas that pass through it freely as samsara. The void may be at leisure while the content molds and shapes itself, when a mental task or project is a "letting be" in the sense that one lets its materials work, more or less, on their own. Like making a clinical diagnosis things are allowed to fall into place and to form their own structure without deliberate interference. This is like letting the requirements of logic determine the logical structure, in impersonal uninvolvement.

Nirvana rides free with no stopping in samsara. Nirvana is in everything and simultaneously transcends everything. Samsara is all that happens on the phenomenological level, nirvana is ground and the unseen forces by which all this happens. Nirvana is like the mind which understands and is the light in which it happens. It has no power in itself, but within it power is represented by interacting forces. One cannot with the mind alone move a pencil, but in the light of the mind the personal mind and personal hand can move it. The mind cannot act on anything; it provides the light and understanding for action. It is in the action, and it transcends the action. The mind enters into thought and it transcends thought at the same time. It is both the inside and the ground of thought. Attention can be focused so that either ground of nirvana is dramatized, or samsara, the working of the differentiations, can be dramatized. In the leisure state the mind is free to alternate and to strike whatever balance it will in nirvana and samsara.

True leisure is beyond entangling involvement with particulars. If particulars are used it is in play rather than work. In Hindu mythology God plays, and the whole world of samsara is created. A particular cannot dominate in true leisure. Leisure is a spirit of abstaining from the serious use of particulars and forms. Only in freedom from particulars can there be relaxation in leisure; there are no directed projects in leisure. Leisure is aimless. This means there must be freedom from habits and compulsions; projects for pleasure or for gain defeat leisure. Leisure is the beginning, process, and the end. There can be nothing to gain, nothing to lose, not even time. Time does not exist in leisure, because time is measured, and all measuring is work oriented. If anything passes, leisure is not there. Leisure does not deal with passing, because it is in the present totality of reality.

If the value of leisure is lost, the value of existence becomes questionable. Both Zen and Heidegger can be easily interpreted as pointing to the need of finding the way back to leisure. During the socialization process we are impressed by the conventions, with the necessity of establishing ourselves by our own achievement, to prove our adequacy as individuals. But we had our existence, in all its abundance in the first place. What good is it to gain the whole world if we lose the sense of Being? If one closes off being, realization, and enlightenment, in light of what is one to appreciate achievement? Achievement is not bad, but if exaggerated focus of attention on achievement causes loss of leisure, the soul is lost. Without leisure there is eventually emptiness, boredom, and the likelihood of harmful and useless habits. We may become conditioned by things rather than by the reality that we are open to originally in our given existence.

To live in the light of Being is to place leisure above work. However, work is necessary for expression in the external world of things. Life has its soft side and its hard side. Leisure is the soft side and work is the hard side. When work gets the upper hand, even striving for pleasure robs one of the true value of pleasure; striving to get pleasure becomes a compulsion. In living in the light of Being, only a few things may be actualized. The greater portion of the life is only realized and not overtly expressed. Existence is given, not earned. There is nothing to push toward unless it is clearly one's duty to push toward it, and duty is mostly projected from the personal mind. The first duty is to take life in its abundance.

From the practical standpoint, leisure may be seen as idleness, but it has nothing whatsoever to do with laziness or lack of industry. In the true spirit of meditation one is disciplined not to squander his energies unnecessarily by becoming entangled in the workings of samsara. Idleness and laziness occur in undisciplined self-indulgence on the ego level, in which the easiest available particulars for selfish ends dominate. Thus, there is desire for some petty, personal gain. Leisure is strictly impersonally motivated; it is a direct working of Being, and what is done is an expression or actualization of Being, and this is done spontaneously without interference by deliberate effort to inhibit or to facilitate the process of realization.

In leisure the mind may be activated in what Kubie refers to as subconscious level, with free interplay of mental phenomena. There is no deliberate guidance toward form and no known purpose. All that arises in the mind is left free to determine its own fate. When something arises enough to take conscious form, it has matured to the point that judgment can be made of it. If it seems worthy to consider the mind may tentatively work on it, but until it meets the criterion for disturbance of leisure, no special work attention is given to it.

True leisure is based on the sufficiency of existence with no special particulars. There is nothing to get, no special desire to be satisfied. Existence as it is naturally happening is valued above all. The attitude is to let being be, what happens, happens, and this is as it should be. The Taoistic Way is the superior way; it requires no choice. There is no picking and choosing. The whole universe taken as a whole can take care of itself, and a person does not need to strain himself to make the universe what it should be. He is only a small part, and his part is clear. If he sees into the nature of things, he has the wisdom of the universe.

The leisure attitude stretches out into nothingness; the work attitude stretches out into the scheduled part of life. The scheduled part of life is that of plans, anticipations, achievement, and all that extends out into the external world. The work side as schedule has to do with the ordering of expected events and keeping them in proper sequence. Activity must follow activity until projects are finished and achievement is satisfactory. Leisure leads to the open aspect of formless realization of the present, which opens up beyond to formless possibilities and expectations.

There is an effortless order in the world, and the purpose of leisure is in letting this order be. There is an aspect of the world which through effort must be structured, and this is the world of work. In the world of effortless order the mind does not have to hold things in place; all continues on its way in wondrous and marvelous perfection. From the body to the end of the world, this spontaneous wisdom guides the world without effort. This is not a world of idleness. The silent interaction in the working of the entire world is in perfect harmony; realization of this brings stillness and peace. All happens as if nothing happens. Alert responsiveness to it in no way interferes with it, rather it brings it to life. Attention, attention, attention to the totality of the world. There is nothing needed and nothing to do in this world; it is the world of silent will which demands nothing but attention. This is the world of suchness.

Is it not man's responsibility to open himself to the world of suchness to determine the kind of structure in his world of arrangement it will support? The world of suchness clearly grants existence according to its own secrets and mysterious workings.

71

Man dwells in this world of suchness by letting be. To this world he can never add one thing or make any contribution. He can be responsive only to dwelling in this world. He stretches out in leisure to this world that has been prepared for him continuously from birth to death, waiting for him and asking nothing but his receptiveness. In the world of arrangement the ego of the conventional level makes itself. Compromises involving losses and gains are necessary according to the relationship with the conventional world. But the active relationship is not for the world of leisure which depends on receptiveness. Whether or not one realizes it he dwells essentially in the world of suchness; this is the condition of his existence. He left this world to become conventionalized, to condition himself for the world of his arrangement, and he frequently forgets to return. This gives him a rootless and alienated existence. The world of suchness is his home to which he can return only through leisure.

The ideal for leisure is complete oneness in the world as suchness. Any degree of self-indulgence or self-stimulation will interfere. Anything that gives pleasure to the body will cause it to receive special attention, and the unity of oneness is distorted or destroyed. The middle path must be followed. If one is hungry or if one has eaten too much, oversmoked, or overindulged in any way the oneness is affected. Buddha declared that a careful balance in the middle course must be followed. If one can see the necessity of training the body for necessary action of work, then he must realize that there is equal reason for "training" the body for leisure. But the necessary training for leisure may prove more difficult because no specific actions are required as in the work skills, for example typing. Rather than tensing up for expansion of energy, one lets go into relaxation for the absorption of energy.

Leisure and work are two essential aspects of existence. When the two aspects are in perfect interaction the highest point of experience is reached, but when they are pulled apart, and the world of work is dominant, we are open to anxiety, guilt, and despair. When we can conduct ourselves in the market place in the calm cloak of leisure, we are in both worlds, and they are one.

In personal existence much depends on a proper balance of work and leisure. A period of leisure should take its place in the day's struggle, but all through the day there is leisure in the degree to which strain is absent. Leisure and work as realization and actualization are continuous. They are the two sides of the creation of life. There is the creation and the created, and in this manner actualization belongs in the process with realization. There is basically the process of creation, and secondarily the thing created or the achievement. The created or the achieved is imagined to be able to stand alone and is thus lost from realization. But that which is created is no more than a part of the process. Realization depends on interaction with achievement. Achievement alone will not give realization, but realization without some kind of achievement is impossible. Each can be seen as the outcome of the other. Leisure can only follow effort. A man is truly the results of his effort. Man is nothing at all until he acts, when he acts his mind observes and there is something for his mind to realize. Realization is fruition of effort which brings leisure.

The realm of being is the ground in which work occurs. Out of being man has carved a man-made culture and conventional reality. Throughout history man has been busy working to develop his tools, communication and transportation, housing, and institutions. This work has occurred within the ground of existence; it is to enrich and assure existence, but modern man has reversed figure and ground so that work and achievement dominate. The little leisure that remains must facilitate and in no way interfere with achievement. Man tries to manage, by means of his work, the total of his existence. He is not content to let being be; he tries to make and control it through his work.

Our civilization has embraced work and left leisure as only a necessary relief from work. We have our coffee break only for the advantage of production, not for the advantage of the man working. Experiments in human engineering are conducted for the improvement of production rather than to improve the quality of work experience of the workers. The ambitious usually get ahead by carrying their work over into nonworking hours, at the expense of true leisure. The advantage gained by our work-dominated culture is that we have made material progress beyond dreams of a few centuries ago, but it is commonly agreed that we have not made similar progress in the development of our human side.

Science has been more helpful in controlling our external environment than in developing our internal environment. Education has become more and more technical and practical. Our universities are primarily for developing intellectual workers.

Education does not develop the individual, even if he emphasizes all possible options open to him. Education is for the conventions of the society and for the conventions of the discipline specialties. No matter what the specialty, it has its rigid conventional thinking and acting. It is up to the individual to go beyond the confines of the discipline to individualize it if he is to work creatively. The development of self is left to chance; there is no place in education or in our marketing-pressuring-advertising society for the values of developing self, and perhaps the majority believes it foolish to develop any aspect of self which might endanger the achievement, work, and efficiency side of the person.

The domination of the achievement motive, with conformity to conventional values, places individuals in competition so that only a very few can achieve the highest levels of success. Since top achievement is the only success the conventionally dominated person can accept, the great majority of people are automatically doomed to failure. As long as there is an appreciable number above one he must consider himself second-rate. However, if self has proper place, and if the diversity of achievement provides for the manifestation of self then competition could be dominated by humanity. Achievement might then advance the cause of humanity.

CHAPTER IX
Meaning and Value

Primarily and ultimately life is the unity of pure experience. Unity first, but within unity, differentiations and integration occur continuously. The unity of the psychic life is experience. Experience in its unity is pure experience; differentiation arises, and from differentiation integration occurs to complete the process. It is important that this unity be seen as continuous throughout experience as differentiations arise and tend toward integrations. Within the continuity of pure experience is the continuity of differentiation and integration. At no place is reality divided, even though the discursive mind may be unconscious of the underlying and enveloping unity. It is important to see pure experience as the unifying principle of individuality, if individuality is to be free from an alienated unity derived from artificially establishing some external boundary that marks it off from life and the world. The individual unit has complete freedom in the self-flowing of its unified experience which encompasses all that arises within it.

Meaning and value are determined in relation to purpose. They arise as reality is differentiated in thought and action. They are impermanent phenomena of interaction as differentiated. Purpose gives preference, meaningful differentiations are made, and the preferred meanings take on value, according to purpose. In conventional achievement orientation, the end result constitutes the chief purpose. Efficiency is required and each differentiation takes on meaning according to its relation to the desired result. In self-realization, understanding is the purpose and differentiations give meanings that lead to understanding. In self-realization all differentiations are values. In self-actualization there is a balance in purpose between understanding and end results.

Purpose determines the way differentiations arise in meaning and value, and if there is no purpose there is no meaningful differentiations. We are pleased and displeased according to our capacity to make differentiations and to set up interactions which move in the direction of our purpose. The purposeless behavior of Zen is for no other purpose than to activate differentiations for the purpose of realization and understanding. This purposeless behavior of Zen is known by the enlightened. If the purpose of behavior is not understood, the unconscious purpose will provide the framework which gives meaning and value, and there will be little understanding of why things have the meaning they have. But as long as differentiations are made there will be some meaning and value.

There is not at first a differentiated world which one learns about and somehow connects himself to through meanings and values. The meanings and values arise with differentiation, determining and being determined with differentiations. Differentiations arise in meaning and value and are integrated in light of purpose. Purpose, as suggested, may be an end in view or purposeless in relation to realization, responsiveness, and leisure. What has been said about there being no differentiated world that has meanings and values assigned to things also applies to self which arises inseparably with the world.

Meaning is cognitive differentiation; value is affective differentiation. There is enough affect in cognitive differentiation to activate it, and there is enough cognition in affective activation to make the differentiation clear. In intellectual work meaning is dominate, the value attribute goes into the ground of intellectual work instead of into the meaningful differentiations. A pure scientist is excited about letting the meanings fall in place in whatever project he is pursuing. In leisure, where there is no purpose beyond realization, meaning and value become one.

Meaning is not to be adequately described because it includes the ground which is beyond conceptualization. Meaning, to be significant, must be sensed beyond what can be objectified. Meaning is to be realized, and this is the reality of meaning. Any meaningful definition of a thing as experience or any description is only an abstract conceptualization. Meaning is subjective, significant, and beyond manipulation. Even though the mind may manipulate a derived conceptualization of meaning, the meaning itself is in the concrete experience. But this concreteness is not an objectified concreteness. Real meaning is meaning that we sense, it is union beyond objectification; i.e., it cannot be the object of thought but is the union of mind and object that is in thought.

Through the process of intellectualization meanings may be abstracted and given value. When abstracted meanings take on value for the individual he attaches himself to these meanings, and they begin to be used in formulating his purpose. In this case, values are left attached in the world to objects that have been differentiated, and they become determinants of behavior. This is the condition in which the individual falls prey to the world of things and forgets Being. The individual thus becomes emotionally attached to the world, and he uses cognition to gain purposes determined by the things he values. He has projected his value into things and cannot freely use the power of valuing independently of things. Old differentiations become statically established with projected meaning and value and reality apparently loses its flowing, self-forming aspect. With meaning and value lodged in old differentiations, new differentiations are slow to appear. With meaning and value attached to old differentiations, purpose becomes primarily a preoccupation with arrangement and re-arrangement of old differentiations. Life begins to lose its significance as meaning, value, and purpose thus becomes limited and bound. Meaning, value, and purpose are differentiations of consciousness and in reality have the same freedom of consciousness.

Boredom occurs when there is no real purpose, but there is usually enough purpose to find a low quality of meaning. The little purpose that remains is for meaning and value which have been left in "things." There is a minimum of meaning and value left in anything which has served in a purposeful project, but left without the context of the purpose, significance is greatly reduced. In boredom there are all the differentiated objects around one that have been useful for past projects, that have had meaning and value, but as there is no purpose for which they are to be activated, they now have low meaning and value. Everything approaches meaninglessness. Purpose serves to activate the process of investing meanings and values in what is useful for the purpose. But meaningful purpose is missing in boredom.

It is clear by now that meaning and value are part of the psychic life of the individual and do not belong to differentiations that are made except as the individual invests meaning and value in these differentiations. When the individual withdraws his interest from objects, no meaning and value remain in them. If an object is valued over and over, day after day, it is because the individual in each encounter re-invests his meaning or his value. To suppose that meaning and value belong to objects, situations, or events motivates the individual to narrow his reality by seeking that which has been meaningful to him in the past. As reality is narrowed the capacity of the individual to create meaning and value is diminished.

The individual is ultimate; all comes back to him in the end. Everything has meaning and value only if the individual gives this meaning and value. Great art, inventions, materials, scriptures, and everything else "lives" only because individuals bring them to "life." Reason, causation, science and technology, or anything else can have no meaning and value except to an individual. Theories are interesting, like checkers or chess, but our reality makes them interesting or disinteresting as the case may be. We arrange things in the human world. We realize and actualize according to our own purpose.

It is the experience and not the object that gives meaning. The object is said to have meaning because it is the encounter with the object that helps to determine the nature of the experience. But the experience is psychological union of the person and the object. The object independent of experience has no meaning and no meaning-giving power. This does not mean that objects are not given conventional meanings which may well influence the activated meaning when the object is encountered. All preconceived notions help to determine meanings, but these preconceived notions may weaken the meaning, since true meaning arises from the experience and is not externally determined.

Meaning is a function of the person in relation with his world.

78

The world of objects has stable characteristics independent of the person which endures according to its own stability. This world is a world without meaning until the person gives it meaning. Since meaning is not in the object, but is a function of the person, it is of the order of consciousness. One is always conscious, but consciousness may continually shift from one thing to another, lighting up each object of its intent. Through its own effort it may remain on one object to the exclusion of others through power of concentration. Exactly the same observation may be made of meaning, with the movement of consciousness goes meaning, being determined like conscious content by intentions and the nature of whatever is being considered. The conventional view which frequently leads to meaninglessness or to low meaning and weakening of motivation, is to believe that meaning lies in things about one. To repeat, meaning exists in no place except in the activation of experience. To look to the object and not in the mind for meaning is a mistake. This does not mean that the mind is free to determine subjectively any meaning it wishes. It means that to the characteristics of qualities of the object must be added meaning which is appropriate to one's own frame of reference. Meaning is in experience and experience is the intentional relation with the object.

The individual is not as much responsible for his meanings and values as he is responsive to them. He is responsible in that they arise in his own reality, and that they arise according to self-forming purposes. The deliberate consciousness is structured through the arising of differentiations with their meanings and values. At the deliberate conscious level they come or appear to one, and, in this sense, the individual is responsive to them. They arise in a leisure state of mind and are taken up and put to work. Responsibility can refer to the use of these differentiations, meanings, and values after they arise. Once they have arisen the consciousness can hold on to them and use them for a deliberate purpose. The idea is not that we accumulate a conscious structure that enables us to fabricate something of significance. We are the capacity which enables us to establish significance in reality as it is constituted each moment, or as it appears in an open mind in reflection and action. We project our intentions and establish our meanings and values. It is in our actualization that we create meaning and value; their creation is part of the process. They are not formulated independently and then worked into the process some way. They arise in our experience as we activate our reality.

Meaning for our personal existence is our way of experiencing understanding, and understanding is realization of the psychological union of our nonsubstantial being with objective and substantial reality. Realization is responsiveness to self-forming meaning of the being side of existence, as it is undifferentiatedly related to existence. Reality is the body, being is the spirit, spirit meaning here whatever man is that enables him to live the kind of psychological life he lives. And life for man is psychological and not physiological, or substantial, or objective, or fixed into some sort of definite thing. This spirit (existence) is not and cannot be known in conceptual terms, at this stage of evolution, and who can say if it can ever be subdued by concepts, or if it is desirable to harness this freedom of existence.

The human world is founded in concern, feeling, meaning, and value. It has been said frequently that man differs most from all other beings in that he has awareness of his awareness, that his knowledge and intelligence make the vital difference. It is our position here that intelligence and knowledge have evolved as chief characteristics of man because he does care enough to give his attention to his experience and to the world with which he is related. And because he does find meaning and value for his existence, life takes on a unique quality for man. Each individual develops his intentional mind according to his own personal motives and emotional predisposition. And for the psychotic there may be a cold world of flatness because he does not care enough to develop adequate meanings and values for phenomena of his world. He may also create an unreal world of his own bizarre making.

One's life is continuous relating to what one is concerned about, and it is hard to imagine a life without concern. This would be an existence in which one is indifferent to all that appears before him. There would be no real point in making any difference or in organizing particulars into clusters for further meaning. There would be no real point in remembering or anticipating things in this way or that. There would be no human life as we know it.

There would be no seeking out or avoiding one thing as opposed to another. This would be an existence without significance and would have no point. It would not even have the purpose of pursuing the everyday life as we know it. Why would such a life have enough purpose to prolong it? This life without concern would be without meaning and value. It is in our feeling, concern, and awareness that meanings and values are differentiated. As we differentiate we determine the meaning and value of what is discriminated. Our world is thus ordered according to the meanings and values that we give our differentiated phenomena.

We have emphasized that purpose is central in determining which differentiations are made. If they are made for knowledge and use, then the meanings and values will be for the end product, for the results. Then eventually all becomes a means and the end is never reached. As Sartre says the For-itself is always lacking, life eventually ends in a failure. If differentiations are made for understanding so that everything is an end in itself, life is always complete; it is not being delayed, and it does not depend on the results.

Thought and action for results call for efficiency, and the heart of efficiency is in stripping away all that does not give the results wanted. There is no motive or time for any extra activation. The more knowledge the more efficiency, the better the plan the more efficiency. All that is learned in the action is the elimination of anything whatsoever that delays results. The closer the results are to the action the more bound the person becomes. Reality is narrowed and much of it is lost from attention.

Individuality is a self-renewing process which continuously realizes itself in experience. There is never any stoppage, never any return, and the only arrival is that which is present at each moment of the process. Always as experience passes, its realizations are fed back into the process to make it ever-forming, always creative. Each moment is not really in addition to, but is more a new coming into being, a birth, but, then, seen this way, the life process is a birth process. It is a process coming into being from what seems to us to be nothingness before our birth, but this birth is also part of the process, and for that matter, so was conception. We lack realization of our process before we were born, and we

81

must admit a lack of full realization of our process during life. We do not own even ourselves; we "happen" as a part of the universal process, and we can never separate ourselves from it. We can only have the illusion that we do. We can have the illusion that we are independent, but we are responsibly interdependent. Thought and motive must be in receptiveness to the field of forces of the universal process.

Obviously, at any time in one's life, one cannot live by past meanings and values. One cannot gain renewal by trying harder to rationalize and revitalize his past values. No, meaning and value must continuously evolve as new self-and-reality is activated in self-formation. This self-forming is a flowing process, and its meanings and values are self-forming. What was will never be again; only in history can it be revitalized, not in life. In the conventional view, one was growing and changing, and one thought he had arrived in adulthood; then he wants to go back because he has lost the greatest meaning there is, growth, a constant value of evolution. There is nothing that can be retained, except constant change and growth. Constant change and growth is the paradise from which one was driven; he was driven out in the Fall, and the Fall is acquisition of conventional knowledge. Man ate from the fruit of the tree of knowledge. Man does not have the knowledge he desires, knowledge of reality. Knowledge of reality is not to be had, because it is present only in the realization of the interaction which is existence. Anything that is crystalized is no longer of the living process; the fruit of the tree of knowledge decays as soon as it is ripe.

One illusion of knowledge is that one grows up. And being grown-up gives the impression that finally the process is fixed, and one continues to deal with things he has gotten or has got the power to get. But knowledge taken out of the process of creative-reality is false knowledge. There is no stopping and no meaning that are not always changing and becoming a different meaning.

With the rapid growth of the physical and intellectual aspects that are largely finished at about twenty to twenty-five years of age, the impression is that man is grown. This means only that one's capacity to deal actively and intellectually with "things" has reached maturity. The truth is that growth takes on more subtle forms, and the nonsubstantial aspects of man begin to grow (or will if man does not interfere) just as rapidly in other directions. In a general way, Jung's concept of individuation describes this shift of growth.

Adult growth has not been obvious, not realized, and, therefore, not cultivated by very many individuals. There is frequently a vague realization that life should have more meaning, and the resourcefulness of man's mind has frequently been able to shore up and support by rationalization and other means his old meanings and values. Even the mystic has only a limited avenue open to him in being focused rather than being diffused throughout the whole life-world. Too frequently, man has blindly limited himself to already discovered meanings and values, whereas the life and growth of the mind are in the continuous creation of meanings and values. For example, man has seen the value of red color as a constant shade, regardless of its value constantly changing in light of the shifting sun and the interplay of the light waves. Man has deadened his responsiveness to the continual flow of reality. If there is any other way, his expectation is for someone to show him, but he is beyond being shown and can only find his own way or be lost in the maze of crystalized and dead meanings and values.

The individual needs to recall that early growth was hard and painful and that there was no easy way. He was constantly driven to tears and to feeling sorry for himself; he had to turn to others for help and love. He desperately wished to be grown so he would not have to face the difficult period of growth. In the first place, this matter of growing up should not have been held out to him as a process which would end, and with its ending all he would have to do would be to enjoy the fruits of his struggle in growing up. The demanding adults that supervised his growing up became too closely identified as reality, and when they were pleased the conditions of reality were assumed to have been met. One would grow up in meeting the conditions he was taught, and that would satisfy reality. Thus, to adjust to the system, to live according to the conventions was equated with the problem of satisfying reality. If the individual awakens in responsiveness to reality, he will see that the growing-up period got him in "training" for the even more

83

difficult task of being his nonsubstantial existence in full partner-
ship with substantial reality.

Throughout the span of life the fundamental questions regarding meaning and value must be re-thought and re-determined. Man
exists in history and the questions as well as the answers change
with the continuous evolution of reality. Within one's life span
his reality is in constant flux as is perfectly obvious in considering
age-appropriateness. Day by day, as one grows, develops, and becomes older (as he passes through life) he cannot hold on to old
meanings. And this is even more noticeable when the social and
technological order is also in rapid change. There must be a continual interaction between changes due to the development of
personal history and the changes in the social-world order. What
is most meaningful today may change tomorrow, and if not by
tomorrow, surely within a few days or months. A child cannot
use a man's values, nor a man a child's values. A child today needs
different values from what he needed the last generation. Always
there is something common from one generation to the next, in
meaning and value, but meaning and value are agents of change
and not left behind.

Meaning and value arise with differentiation. Of differentiation
there is no end; differentiation within pure experience is the life
of the mind. To focus altogether on differentiations and to worry
oneself exclusively about results are what in Taoism is called chasing
the beast of the field. To realize one's true place as pure experience
in which particulars occur with their impermanent meanings and
values freely arising with all things in their place may be a kind
of ultimate purpose which the unenlightened unconsciously seek
and the enlightened consciously realize. The mind is always populated with thoughts and feelings with their meaning and value just
as the world is populated with particulars. And the thoughts and
feelings of the mind interact with the particulars of the world.

CHAPTER X

Psychotherapy

So far we have been considering the individual making himself as a human and discovering himself as a being. The better understanding one has of individuality the more certain it seems that the individual must develop his unique constellation by his own efforts. In psychotherapy another person undertakes the task of helping the individual form himself.

Psychotherapy immediately faces a dilemma, because if individualization depends on one's own efforts, then anything that might be done for the individual denies him the benefits of making himself by his effort, and if it does not weaken him, robs him of opportunity. The task then of psychotherapy is not to do anything directly for the individual but to help him to activate himself. The therapist cannot go behind the scene of actualization and lay any groundwork or indicate direction. The wisdom, intuition, understanding, and knowledge of the therapist are of no use to the other person. If the client is to be helped it must be at the level of the source of his existence so that he finds his own wisdom, uses his own intuition to reach his own understanding and knowledge. The therapist cannot help by giving cues; the client must find his own clues to guide him. The help of the therapist is somewhat like the Zen master who says, "If you have a staff, I will give it to you; if you have no staff, I will take it away."

It is as difficult to say how therapy is to be done as it is to say how life is to be lived. Therefore, the literature on how to do therapy stands in the same relationship to therapy as the literature on how to live stands in relationship to living. The use will depend upon the ingenuity of the user. The chief difficulty in using verbalization about therapy as a guide is that, like life, much of it is beyond the level of verbalization. This is recognized in that training requires supervised practice. Therapy is definitely an art. It is an art with a living result. Its product is not finished but emerges as a living self-creating process. This should be the supreme work of art, and its product should be the creative process of the client's individuality.

Views of therapy as a rule are too limited. An adequate view cannot be strictly subjective, objective, or phenomenological because it must transcend any single viewpoint. All of these represent views that many people take in conceptualizing their reality. The view taken will determine the kind of reality that is differentiated in meanings and values. The therapist can exclude no possible view, and he must be open to all possibilities. Obviously all possible views are not known; therefore, the therapist cannot say that a newly created view of any particular person is unrealistic because it does not agree with anything that he already knows. In the same line of consideration the therapist cannot prepare himself by knowing what is a proper way to deal with reality in thought, fantasy, action, or realization. The therapist obviously cannot know all possible views, and he must be prepared to understand a new view and to work creatively with it in his interaction with the client. How many individuals in the past have suffered because of a true view of reality which disagreed with the conventional view and with the best authorities? Frequently in history the individual was right and the authority was wrong. How often does a therapist in this manner place the forward looking individual under even a greater strain by inability of the therapist to see the client's truth when it represents an unusual view?

This discussion of psychotherapy is not to present a design for therapy or even a systematic approach. Rather the purpose is to encourage reflection on some usually neglected aspects of the process. At this point in the development of therapy it might even be healthy to call to question the idea of design and systematic approach. Most people working at therapy have taken over and are attempting to apply what they are convinced are relatively objective approaches. Indeed, using a conventional approach to therapy can very well give false security which blinds the therapist to the inadequacy of his practice. Doing therapy by another person's theory is like trying to live by the directions of another. Buddha referred to one using the thoughts of others as a herdsman of other men's cows. Mohammed compares it with an ass bearing a load of books. It is argued by the authorities in the field of psychotherapy that the use of established theories lends validity to therapy. Also, who has adequately developed his own understanding so as to be able to work in therapy in the light of the reality of existence? The intention here is to bring up the idea that psychotherapy is a possibility, but it cannot be done merely by passing a routinely prescribed course of formal training, which admittedly is a necessary beginning. Every psychotherapist should be more impressed with what he does not know about the mind than with what he does know; this should be seen as his greatest asset and perhaps the source of successful therapy rather than what he thinks he knows. One difficulty of depending altogether on what is known is that it leads to a tendency to manipulate.

Therapy occurs in the interaction of the two people involved in it. Part of its results is reflected in the behavior of the client. This part of its results is the purpose of therapy. The results should not be seen simply as a change that comes about after so many therapy sessions, rather the results should begin to be present immediately in the first session as it is fed back into the experience of the client in his therapy session. The results will be a continuous determinant of further change. The results of therapy are a dynamic process from the beginning of therapy. The client does not necessarily need to be conscious of this result-process in any particular way or perhaps not at all, but the therapist must give it careful attention. He must ask himself primarily what results he sees occurring in the therapy process itself rather than focus on what the results may be outside of therapy. It is only in the therapy session that the therapist can see the results directly; otherwise he has only the reports of abstractions for it if he looks for it in reports by the client of changes in outside life.

Any outside change should be seen as secondary gain; it plays no direct role in the therapy session. Life calls for response to immediately present reality first of all, and this is to add up to whatever projects of achievement and behavior that the immediate experience makes possible. Life has its origin in immediate experience and not in some other hypothetical position. This does not mean that one is under the pleasure principle, because the present adequately contains reality of the past and the future when ongoing projects stand in adequate openness in the present. One may work and actualize for tomorrow, but first he must live and realize for today. If each experience as it is present cannot be fully realized (more accurately the stream of experience that is continuously present) the total may add up with one being president of his club, but he will not have lived and will not know how to live. The first aim of therapy must be concerned with depth and quality of experience, rather than primary consideration being given to where this is leading. Therapy is to learn how to live and not how to win a prize. Therapy is living, not preparing to live, as one sits safely removed from life in a sheltered counseling room with a permissive atmosphere. Its immediate results are its most profound results.

It must be emphasized that the therapy session must be one of direct living; the client is brought ever closer to his experience. He at first talks of them from afar, as though he really does not mean to do what he does, and as though he is not satisfied with his experience. He is having the experiences because he cannot have better ones, and he is not at all happy about having them. He does not want to recognize that he is essentially his experience; he is trying to alienate himself from them, but he cannot do it. The chief purpose is to accept the act, the experience that is now here as the reality that the client has been looking for all along. The therapy session is a lesson in living. However much the person may be deceived, existence offers nothing greater than the reality which is present. If sorrow is present one must be sorrowful, if happiness is present then one must be happy. If one is in trouble and must suffer, then he lives in suffering. When it rains one gets wet, when it is sunny one is warm. To try to escape reality in wanting something else puts one in a suspended and alienated state.

There is danger that the individual who goes to the therapist for help because he is losing ability to run his life may come to feel displaced altogether. To the extent the therapist takes over, the client is displaced and is no longer central even in his own life. This is like a small country that is in danger of losing its independence going to another for help and the one it goes to taking over. A therapist must remember that he is an outsider, a handy man who has been called in to help. A therapist is in the employment of the client and should not attempt to tell the client what to do. The client may be in trouble, but he is still the employer and not the employed. He is a free man with the freedom inherent in his existence. It is bad enough to be displaced in one's external world, but to have one's own individuality taken over by another is too much. The therapist is company and must not take over. The individual is king in his own life. He is still running it or letting it run down. He is responsible. Whatever the case, it is up to the individual. A therapist is a guest in the existence of the client as long as the client thinks the therapist has something to offer. The therapist is no more than this unless the client makes him more.

The therapist does not follow technics; rather, he depends on a broad approach, the same approach with which he faces life. From the union in the therapeutic situation differentiations arise, are manifested in meanings and values, are interrelated with other differentiations, and integrated into a synthesis. In this type of creative process the therapist is primarily responsive, in a leisure state, but he is an extremely careful observer who also acts as a very real part of the reality of the therapeutic union. Form is sought, utilized, but not allowed to enslave. The reality of the therapeutic situation is activated, much of this reality will come in the activation of the client. The phenomena of his mind, thoughts, feelings, impressions, meanings, values, and whatever differentiations appear are examined and experienced for their reality. Life is creative, and therapy should free the person to be creative in his living. Flexibility, options in meanings and values, exploration of possibilities, new interpretations that the client might find will all help to open up the system in freedom for creative living. Switch of point of view, change of context, finding new relationships, and more versatile meanings of his reality will also help. The therapist is to help the client see the flow of things, see the patterns of reality, and take responsibility for what he is and what he is becoming, in a creative way.

Therapy is a process of helping the individual activate himself more suitably at whatever level and in whatever direction he is struggling to achieve his individuality. As this is in the light of being, the inter-relationship of his actualization in the light of being must be discovered in a way which is appropriate to him. The therapist joins in compassionately with the individual to help him constitute his individuality in the ground of his existence.

Any efforts to help an individual in psychotherapy should be in light of the full potentials of individuality. The wide possibility of points of view which may be legitimately taken must be recognized. Each individual has his own inner reality to which only he has access and which can be expressed only within the limits of verbalization or direct action. This inner reality is available to the individual through direct realization. What he can represent in verbalization or in direct action is the self-actualization side of his existence. The individual's inner experience must be realized and incorporated into his identity, and since realization of this side of his existence is experienced directly and is not to be known or revealed in any other way, it must be self-validated. There can be no external criterion for it. Self-realization is dependent on responsiveness to existence and self-actualization is dependent on responsible efforts to actualize oneself as a person. Individual reality is free and creative, but in the active side of life much of one's actions must be focused through the available conventional forms. Within one's existence thought and action determine differentiations with their meanings and values. This is a summary of the continuous process of individuality, and the task of the therapist is to activate and stimulate this process wherever and however he can.

An elementary observation about therapy is that it is on the self level and not on the ego level. This is what is usually referred to as depth or basic personality factors, with outward form being considered as symptoms. Therapy has typically been directed to the unconscious, to help the individual gain insight into his unconscious mechanisms. But too often this has been an outside approach, such that the unconsciousness is to be interpreted in terms of the conscious structures. It has been our argument here that much of the unconscious is a source and that much of it can never be anything but source. Conscious concepts are not made conscious in the sense that there was form within, but in the sense that expression from within gives form. Actualization is action in light of realization and understanding that is beyond knowledge, and it does not come from the realm of what is already actualized. It is not the product of reason from what has already been formulated, except that what has already been formulated has come from the inner reality.

One cannot prove one's self-realization to others; what one realizes is not to be seen by any other person, it cannot be objectified, it cannot be expressed. One can feel it in expression but it remains beyond the expression as ground. The best one can do is self-actualization. This is expression which does not violate realization, is made in the light of realization. One's self-actualization will be judged by others in the conventional framework. It will be realization to the individual, but it will have the conventional achievement view to others. One may be highly successful in activating his authentic realization and have authentic expression for it. But it is judged externally by others. To hope for more is to expect the unreasonable.

The client may think he depends on consensual validation. But it is self-validation that he actually wants. He thinks he has to be approved by others before he can approve of himself. This is a mistake. He is convinced he cannot validate himself on the level of self and experience because he cannot get validation on this level from others. This is asking too much from others, that they give approval on the level of quality of experience. It is like depending on someone to tell you how you feel. One is self-conscious because he has not proven himself to others and therefore not to himself. One wants self-confidence but he makes it depend on what he does before others. It is argued one is impressed by what others see him as being. But one is not any good to others unless he is self-validated.

The client's validation problem is central for therapy. His life is not working as he feels it should. There is something wrong, and there being something wrong is due to invalid sense of being or lack of effective actualization. The more that goes wrong the more uncertain and confused he is likely to become and the more questionable his behavior becomes. His results do not validate his behavior nor do others validate it. The way he is differentiating aspects of his existence and his distorted meanings and values add to his confusion. It is the task of the therapist to help the individual sense validation of his experience and to find convincing meaning for his differentiations.

Therapy is centered on the client's efforts in self-actualization. Existence is given. The client is open in realization to the possibilities of existence. His trouble arises in actualizing these possibilities. He cannot seem to actualize himself in a way that is representative and worthy of his realization. His frustration grows and even realization of himself becomes confusing and he is alienated from it. His failures in self-actualization rob him of his self-realization. He loses discrimination of realization and actualization. If he can again distinguish between these two major modes of individuality and gain self-validation in realization, he can gain patience for efforts in self-actualization. Self-realization can give the security necessary for delayed actualization and reestablish hope. The possibilities given with existence are real possibilities and confidence is generated. Thus, the first step in therapeutic movement toward actualization is reestablishment in realization. The client can regain his self-validation and again believe in himself. It is frustrating that he is not able to gain consensual validation for his efforts in living, but he has the validation from the therapist for his actualization in the therapy session. This is the foundation for his renewed efforts to actualize himself more authentically.

Therapy must not be seen as only another human endeavor in the affairs of men. It is not to be guided by external criteria. There are no external criteria. There are no external criteria for either the process or the outcome. External symptoms are only by-products. Many therapists would object to this statement, because they have hopes of scientifically validating psychotherapy. But obviously therapy is as open as life and there is too much of it beyond formulated reality to expect to submit more than formal aspects of outcomes of therapy to current research methods. There can no more be a preconceived pattern for therapy than there can be for life. Therapy must not become like other human endeavors in that once action is anticipated it must be governed by demands and requirements on the level of the already actualized. Therapy is too complex and lies too much in the area of possibility to be governed by actualities. Therapy is a possibility which may be actualized under favorable conditions.

Therapy like life can be very difficult. But the impossible of the moment is most worth working toward. The answer does not yet exist, not even the question. How can one say how a free process such as the individual will or should be? How can the therapist and client work toward what it is to be, most essentially, if the most essential is not known? Life or therapy can be extremely intricate, both are worthy of full attention, both are extremely fascinating. Realization of the complexities involved has nothing to do with a whimpering despair or a blocking frustration. It calls for a full appreciation of whatever can be actualized in any form it can be brought forth. At times the least phenomenon has the greatest significance. When phenomena are all about one and the void is filled with teeming activation, appreciation goes to all, but it is in the poverty and scarceness that the full power of the mind and the person is called upon to find significance and to keep the full process going until it is again teeming with phenomena.

One cannot live adequately or do adequate therapy without full commitment to reality. Reality can be trusted if one will stay directly in touch with it through care, intent, commitment, and involvement. This is man's contribution as he stands in the light of the mind. He can bring about all that is brought about in human reality. There is no room to waver; there is room for realization, responsiveness, and leisure but not for uncertainty and hesitancy after reality has been revealed. Then is the time for responsibility for actualization.

Of all the professions psychotherapy probably demands more of the total activation of the person, that is, full and whole development. This certainly does not imply that the personal development of any professional man is not important, but most professions depend primarily on a special development of proficiency for successful achievement. Psychotherapy too demands specialization, but when it comes to therapy more depends on a wide range of activation of the person himself than what a speciality implies. The speciality concerns the whole of the existence of man. Most professions demand proficiency in service as foremost, therapy places humanness above efficiency, and this humanness requires nothing less than the full development of the whole person. The humanness of the therapist is at the source of his efficiency. The The therapist "uses" himself as his primary instrument of service.

As a person the therapist should be expanding his identity to include the whole man; the more of himself he has activated the more responsive he is to the wide range of experience he is called upon to explore with his clients. He most definitely should not be a person who has gained his personal fulfillment by limiting his life to what he can handle comfortably by turning to the positive and avoiding the negative. He must be extending himself to the limits of his potentials. For with anything less the therapist cannot properly appreciate the intense struggle the client faces. To reach the limits of potentialities is an unconscious drive of all persons, but in the therapist it must be conscious. And as one concerned with the full range of human experience he should be familiar with the part that negative experiences and adverses have played in the history of man and in the life of each individual. He cannot afford to spare himself what is so central to human existence.

The therapist must have full understanding of and appreciation for the negative aspects of life. This means primarily as experienced by the person and not merely as knowledge of diagnostic categories (but certainly he will have this knowledge). It is because of the negative aspect of life that the client is in trouble, or it could be put the other way, that the client cannot find sufficient satisfaction in the positive realm of life. And for the human when there is not light there is darkness. The therapist needs to understand the full range of suffering, struggle, guilt, shame, frustration, anxiety, and all the negative sides of life. The shadow or dark side must be understood firsthand by the therapist; it is not enough that he has abstract knowledge of this. But at the same time, the therapist cannot be dominated by human miseries; he must not be under their oppressive limitations. In clients, he sees much misery, much frustration, and only a small amount of satisfaction, and he must live with this because it is at the foundation of his work with others who are in trouble. Human trouble and misery are his business, and he must understand and realize what he is most concerned about. He must draw upon his own experience in frustrations, and his compassion for himself in such struggle can be transferred to all other living persons.

Troubles and sorrows are realities of life. The therapist rapidly becomes exposed to these in his work; instead of avoiding them personally he must realize them as fully as he can. He must put himself in the other person's situation and feel as the other person does as deeply as he can. But he must not be trapped within these experiences. He must be able to transcend the personal without losing the slightest personal significance of each particular. He must be able to reduce universal and impersonal understanding to the personal and be able to see the personal as universal and impersonal. However, if he cannot become personally involved then the impersonal is only objective impersonality. The therapist experiences himself as deeply personal as he can and expands this into universality, to reach the point where he experiences his own concerns as being universal and to be held in common to all men. The therapist must come to share the feelings of all mankind. Any trouble of another person or of all people throughout the world is shared by the therapist. He is more human than he is a person. He leaves the confines of his petty personal life and loses himself in Self that he may gain universality.

The background of the therapist needs to be broad enough to enable him to understand the full range of human experience. He need not have had all specific experiences of mankind, but he needs to understand that they are a possibility for him. He must be open to the range of experience, and he must have the capacity to go to the depth or source of particular experiences. The particular arises from pure experience, and the therapist must be thoroughly grounded in pure experience. Whatever turns up in experience, no matter what the particular may be, the therapist can see its dominant place as a particular and can simultaneously put it in perspective. Thus, he has full appreciation of the "birth and death" of the impermanent aspect of the fleeing experience of man. He can participate in the particular fully while at the same time transcending to be identical with the stable and unchanging pure experience. The impermanent passing experience is not minimized because the whole is understood, rather it takes on the significance of the whole. The whole universe crawls with the struggling ant.

Psychotherapy is intensified living in the depths of experience. The closer the therapist is to his ground of existence the more effectively he can activate therapeutic experience in the client.

Bibliography

Barrett, William (ed.). *Zen Buddhism: Selected Writings of D. T. Suzuki.* New York: Doubleday Anchor, 1956.

Bronowski, J. *The Identity of Man.* New York: The Natural History Press, 1965.

Buber, Martin. "The Place of Hasidism in the History of Religion." In William Briggs, *Anthology of Zen.* New York: Evergreen Books, 1961.

Heidegger, Martin. *Existence and Being.* Chicago: Regnery, 1949.

Huxley, Aldous. *Tomorrow and Tomorrow and Tomorrow and Other Essays.* New York: The American Library, 1964.

Jung, C. G. *Modern Man in Search of a Soul.* Translated by W. S. Dell and Cary F. Baynes. New York: Harcourt, Brace Company, 1933.

Kapleau, Philip (ed.). *The Three Pillars of Zen.* New York: Harper and Row, 1966.

Kubie, Lawrence S. *Neurotic Distortion of the Creative Process.* New York: Noonday Press, 1961.

Nishida, Kitaro. *Intelligibility and the Philosophy of Nothingness.* Translated by Robert Schinzinger. Tokyo: Maruzen, 1958.

Northrop, F. S. C. *The Meeting of East and West.* New York: Macmillan, 1950.

Pieper, Josef. *Leisure: The Basis of Culture.* Translated by Alexander Dru. New York: The New American Library, 1963.

Rogers, Carl R. *On Becoming a Person.* Boston: Houghton Mifflin, 1961.

Sartre, Jean-Paul. *Being and Nothingness.* Translated by Hazel E. Barnes. New York: The Citadel Press, 1965.

Unamuno, de, Miguel. *Tragic Sense of Life.* Translated by J. E. Crawford Flitch. New York: Dover Publications, 1954.